> *Adieu, adieu, adieu,*
> *Remember me.*
>
> William Shakespeare
Hamlet
Act I, Sc. v, line 91

Death & the Fear of Finiteness in Hamlet

Jerome Oremland M.D.

LAKE STREET EDITIONS

DEDICATION AND ACKNOWLEDGEMENTS

This book is dedicated to my dear friend Barbara Young Bracket who introduced our family to the satisfactions to be found in Shakespeare's words. More than that she helped our family appreciate the infinite beauty of the English language.

My son, Noah, acted nearly as co-author of this book. His insights added greatly to my ideas. His careful reading and criticism of the manuscript strengthened it immeasurably. Celia Teter was our editor. Her unfailing attention to detail made for accuracy in the writing and in the quotes. It is due to her skill that Noah's and my complex syntax became readable.

I owe a great deal to Mark Murphey, a leading actor with the Oregon Shakespeare Festival. Mark's 1974 Horatio, his 1983 remarkable portrayal of the tragic prince, and his friendship have quietly encouraged me in this pursuit.

Copyright © 2005 by Jerome D. Oremland, M.D.
All rights reserved. No part of this book may be reproduced in any form without written permission from the publisher.

Library of Congress Cataloging-in-Publication Data

Oremland, Jerome D.
    Death and the fear of finiteness in Hamlet / Jerome Oremland.
        p. cm.
    Includes bibliographical references and index.
    ISBN 0-9763968-0-7
1. Shakespeare, William, 1564-1616. Hamlet. 2. Hamlet (Legendary character) 3. Infinite in literature. 4. Death in literature. 5. Fear in literature. 6. Finite, The. I. Title.
PR2807.O74 2005
822.3'3--dc22

                              2005044076

Printed in the USA
Cover and interior design by EudesCo. | www.eudesco.com
10 9 8 7 6 5 4 3 2 1

Lake Street Editions
1134 Lake Street
San Francisco, California 94118
Jdoremland@aol.com

Contents

Foreword vii

Chapter 1. *Hamlet* **and Hamlet** 1
    2. Cain and Abel 9
    3. Gertrude: Queen, Wife, and Mother 23
    4. Laertes, Horatio, Fortinbras, and Hamlet 37
    5. Madness and Hamlet 51
    6. Ophelia and Psychosis 83
    7. Death and Hamlet 93
    8. Existentialism and Psychosis 111

References 117
Line Index 123
Index 135

Foreward

In 1983 while my mother was dying, I was moved to write a chapter for a monograph of *Psychoanalytic Inquiry*, "Themes of Death and Mourning in Art and Literature." My thoughts at the time easily moved to *Hamlet*, a play that rotates around death. In that early work, as I traced the responses to death of the major characters, I identified the Hamlet and Fortinbras dyad as a dramatization of the vicissitudes of identification, an unconscious response to death. Long fascinated by the enhancement and enrichment of the self that identifications produce, I advanced Fortinbras as the personification of unconflicted identification with the lost father—that through identification Fortinbras carries his father within and realizes his father's life. Fortinbras becomes the king of Denmark. Reluctantly, I concluded that Hamlet represented a failure of identification, a conclusion I now see as feeble.

Also central to understanding *Hamlet* and an area of psychoanalytic investigation that has long occupied me are the psychodynamics of psychosis, particularly schizophrenia. Having spent countless hours with people (and their families) who were on the verge of, caught in the abyss of, and reconstituting from schizophrenia, I came to understand the terrifying experience of schizophrenia as existential anxiety—a manifestation of self-fragmentation and impending dissolution of the self. Intuitively I felt a compelling parallel between existential anxiety and the fear of death—the inevitable dissolution of the self into nonexistence. Considering the fear of death as the fear of nonexistence, it seemed clear that, as a high-level unconscious defense, identification protects us from recognizing the finiteness of the self and limits our awareness of the full meaning of death.

The realization of death as the finiteness of self painfully became clear to me during the dying of my dear wife, Evelyn. Her death forced upon me once again thoughts of the Prince of Denmark, his fellow players, and the panoply of responses to death that they dramatize.

From the standpoint of understanding responses to death in *Hamlet*, the *To be or not to be* soliloquy is pivotal. Here Hamlet is in the nadir of his struggle between the profound realization that death marks finiteness and the more easily accepted idea that death is another state of being, a *shuffled off... mortal coil*. I suggest that his experience of self-fragmentation following the confrontation with the ghost moves Hamlet to an exquisite appreciation of the fragility and the preciousness of the sense of being. Viewed this way, Hamlet's psychosis takes on new meaning and its essentialness to the progression of the play becomes evident.

With progressive reintegration following the distant, almost mystical, confrontation with Fortinbras, Hamlet evolves an acceptance of the finiteness of the self that is given voice in the dialogues in the Graveyard Scene. His final utterance, *The rest is silence*, reveals Hamlet's clear acceptance of the finiteness of death.

In short, in the arc of the play through the soliloquies, we are taken into thoughts that we dare not think. With Hamlet we travel from self-loathing and a wish for death, *O, that this too too solid flesh would melt*, to a struggle to understand existence, *To be or not to be*, to an acceptance of the inevitability of the finiteness of the self, *The rest is silence*.

Running as subtext in *Hamlet* is the Passion of Christ with marked parallels, marks that were obvious to the Elizabethan mind and are available to the modern. In the final scenes of the play, the striking parallel between Jesus's vision of His destiny and Hamlet's is made visible. Within both lies a paradox, the nature of which is revealed to the reader in the last chapter.

♚ JDO

Hamlet and Hamlet

The structure and story line that William Shakespeare develops in *Hamlet* (1601) are so well known to readers of English literature that they need not be reviewed here. Yet, unpacking the meanings, themes, and implications of *Hamlet* remains infinite. As with any masterpiece, the more that *Hamlet* is studied the more compelling it becomes (Oremland, 1981, 1997).

Although constructed as a revenge tragedy, on an elemental level the play pivots on confrontations with death. L.C. Knights (1960) notes, "Hamlet is living death in the midst of life" (p. 192). C.S. Lewis (1942) writes, "The subject of *Hamlet* is death . . . (in other plays) they think of dying . . . in *Hamlet* we are kept thinking about being dead" (p. 215).

During the course of the play we witness the death of the father, mother, son, sister, brother, uncle, lover, esteemed advisor, friends, and the titular character. The play makes visible humankind's responses to and fear of death (Oremland, 1983). In its exploration of these themes, the play in essence is existential and timeless.

FREUD, *HAMLET*, AND CREATIVITY

The study of *Hamlet* as a complex play and Hamlet as a complex character began in the late eighteenth century with Johann von Goethe (1785) (Hoy, 1963). Goethe saw Hamlet as an esthetic, philosophically inclined man who was ill fitted to the morally repugnant task that had been thrust upon him. For Goethe *Hamlet* was a study of an "action laid upon a soul unfit." Goethe evoked the image of an acorn being planted in a delicate vase and its growth causing the vase to crack. This "cracked vase" reading of the play, although strongly laced with ideas of constitutional "weaknesses," reflected a paradigmatic change in thinking as regards character and personality development. Goethe's views are part of Western culture's embracing the Enlightenment in its struggle to free itself from medieval constructs. Goethe changed the understanding of the play from a revenge tragedy to that of a man in conflict, a study of personality.

Some 100 years later, Sigmund Freud began the modern understanding of psychological conflict and personality. Even in Freud's earliest explorations, *Hamlet* has a conspicuous place.[1] Rather than seeing Hamlet as a man in conflict with his nature, Freud saw Hamlet as a man paralyzed by unconscious desires and fears. Overly narrowly, Freud saw Hamlet's conflict as residing in the developmental triangle that confronts and shapes the psyche of Western man—the Oedipal conflict—the unconsciously continuing infantile wish for and fear of infantile sexualized love of the mother and the unconsciously continuing infantile wish to eliminate and fear of eliminating the father. In Freud's view, Claudius did what Hamlet unconsciously wished to do—kill his father and sexually possess his mother. From Freud's view, it is the unconscious psychical identity between Claudius and Hamlet that renders Hamlet unable to act. In Freud's words, "How can one explain . . . his hesitation to avenge his father by killing his uncle . . . than by the torment roused in him by the obscure memory that he himself had meditated the same deed against his father because of passion for his mother . . . his conscience is his unconscious feeling of guilt" (p. 227).

Freud's views on *Hamlet* have significance beyond the study of the play. Embedded in Freud's thoughts are two powerful paradigms for the exploration of creativity. Freud showed that the psychoanalytic study of art works can augment the biographical study of creative

---

1 On the 15th of October, 1897, in a letter to his colleague Wilhelm Fleiss, Freud mentioned the Oedipus complex. He wrote, "The idea has passed through my head that the same thing (the Oedipus conflict) may lie at the root of *Hamlet*. I am not thinking of Shakespeare's conscious intentions, but supposing rather that he was impelled to write it . . . because his own unconscious understood that of his hero" (p. 227, 1910). These thoughts were elaborated in Freud's most important book, *The Interpretation of Dreams* (1900), in which he used Hamlet to illustrate the Oedipal conflict. Following Freud, Ernest Jones (1949) further developed Freud's ideas into his book, *Hamlet and Oedipus*.

individuals and can supplement art historical and literary studies.

As a study in biography and creativity, Freud noted that Shakespeare wrote *Hamlet* following the death in 1596 of his young son Hamnet and the more recent death of his father John in 1600 or 1601.[2] Freud reasoned that writing *Hamlet* was part of Shakespeare's mourning the death of his son and his father. From this base mark Freud developed a paradigm for understanding a motivation for creativity that he later refined as the specific role that mastery in general and mourning in particular play in various aspects of creativity (Freud, 1917; Pollock, 1975; Oremland, 1980, 1983, 1984).

The Freudian paradigm relates loss and creating and provides a link between significant events in the life of creative individuals and the contents of creativity.[3] At times this paradigm has been distorted to suggest that mourning causes creativity. In actuality, Freud was describing how for creative persons mourning may determine the contents of creativity.

Freud coined the term *pathography* to refer to the study of creative individuals by viewing their art and lives from a psychoanalytic perspective. A better term, *psychoanalytic biography*, comes from Mary Gedo (1980). Psychoanalytic biography was refined in Freud's monograph on Leonardo da Vinci (1910). For 100 years, this model has been fruitfully mined by a host of psychoanalytic biographers in the study of creative individuals (Eissler, 1971; Freud, 1917; Gedo, J., 1983; Greenacre, 1957; Kris, 1952; Liebert, 1982; Pollock, 1975; Rose, 1980).

Although Freud's study of *Hamlet* is of an art work, his most elaborate psychoanalytical study of a work of art was his essay, *The Moses of Michelangelo* (1914). In this essay, the prototypical psychoanalytical

---

2 As with most of the plays, the writing of *Hamlet* cannot be precisely dated; however, Alfred Rowse (1963) dates it at 1600–1601, and Harold Jenkins (2002) squarely dates it in 1601.

The death of Hamnet may even be more clearly represented in *King John*, written in 1596. Constance, mother of Arthur, nephew of John, laments,

>   **Constance:** *Grief fills the room up of my absents child,*
>   *Lies in his bed, walks up and down with me,*
>   *Puts on his pretty looks, repeats his words,*
>   *Remembers me of all his gracious parts,*
>   *Stuffs out his vacant garments with his form*
>   (Act III, Sc. iv)

3 Freud's proposition is in keeping with his statement in the Preface to *The Interpretation of Dreams*, in which he stated that the writing of the book was an important component in the mourning of his father.

study of a work of art, Freud attempted to unpack the many meanings embedded in Michelangelo's statue. To advance this paradigm, Freud used ideas paralleling his studies of dreams and dream formation.

THE DREAM AND WORKS OF ART

In *The Origins and Psychodynamics of Creativity* (1997), I suggested that useful analogies can be drawn between creating and dreaming and between the art work and the dream. When viewed psychoanalytically, inconsistencies, ambiguities, and non sequiturs in art, as in the dream, frequently reveal remarkable latent interpretable meaning. Psychoanalytically, these inconsistencies, ambiguities, and non sequiturs are condensations of multilayered representations of feelings and ideas that are compacted into the imagery.

Condensation

The concept of *condensation* is derived from Freud's topographic model of mental functioning and implies depth and overlay, a metaphoric psychic layering. Art images, like dream images, are seen as composite representations of ideas, emotions, and symbols that coexist on different levels within the image. Condensation parallels the art historical term *typology*—overlaid images that convey multiple meanings.[4]

In studying images, condensation contrasts with ambiguity. Although ambiguity has several meanings, ambiguity generally implies the capacity of being understood in multiple ways (Empson, 1947; Oremland, 1997). Smoke dreams, cloud formations, and Rorschach Ink Blots are ambiguities. No meanings reside within them. The meanings exist within the viewer as projected onto the forms. In contrast the image in an art work is within the image. Like the image in a dream, the image in a work of art is a composite of ideas, emotions, and symbols that coexist (are condensed) on different levels. The meanings are within the images.

---

[4] Because of the importance of dream formation as a model for understanding condensation, condensation may seem overly related to visual images. However, in literature, particularly in poetry and drama, which are closely related to the plastic arts in their capacity to evoke and use visual imagery, condensation is a powerful concept for understanding levels of meaning.

The most erudite study of the evolution of *Hamlet* can be found in Eleanor Prosser's *Hamlet and Revenge* (1971). Prosser advances that it was during the English Restoration following the accession of Charles II to the throne that the conflicted young prince we enjoy today came into being. In a detailed way she traces the changes in the play as various critical, directional, and artistic interpretations were incorporated over the years. As impressive as her research is, I suggest that she does not enough emphasize that the changes are largely the result of directors, actors, critics, and audiences finding new and different meanings within the play. In a sense each time a company selects to perform *Hamlet* it is creating a new play, but each play as created is a selected and organized intensification of meanings residing within the play.[5][6] This is particularly apparent to anyone who watches or reads the play over time. As our experience changes, the play changes. In effect, for the past 400 years directors, actors, critics, audiences, and readers have been unpacking Shakespeare's condensations.

ART INTERPRETATION AND DREAM INTERPRETATION

The process of inferring and sorting meanings is called *interpretation*. Psychoanalytic interpretation of art works is a highly specialized discipline that complements a specific sector of art historical interpretation. Psychoanalytic interpretation of art works draws many parallels from dream interpretation and is related to art appreciation, a term capturing the sense of subjective, nonverbal responses (Oremland, 1984, 1989).

Psychoanalytic interpretation of art works, like psychoanalytic interpretation of dreams, is not projecting onto the images but is the discovering of the condensed meanings within the images. Yet in psychoanalytic interpretation of art works and dream interpretation, the initial response is heavily laced with projection. In both, a refining process develops.

---

5 Of course, I am only considering the important versions of the play that have developed from serious study. There have been innumerable ridiculous adaptations developed for all sorts of reasons that have little to do with the play itself.

6 In describing the rehearsal process of a play's development, Carey Perloff (1997), artistic director of the American Conservatory Theater, San Francisco, notes, "In a creative rehearsal, ideas are traded quickly and freely. They metamorphose and evolve, are shaped and discarded. 'Happy accidents' litter the rehearsal room. Left behind are numerous little plays . . ." as the director and actors struggle to find meaning within any play and to present a cohesive presentation of that found meaning (Oremland, 1997, p. 133).

In psychoanalytic interpretation of art works, as the piece "speaks" to the interpreter responses are evoked. A unique reciprocity develops between the piece and the viewer with the viewer continuously correcting his or her perceptions by returning to the art work and reacting to the gestalt and the details.[7] From this view, psychoanalytic interpretation of works of art becomes a kind of dialogue between the viewer's and the artist's conscious and unconscious guided by the images.

In dream analysis the process is parallel. Initially the dream interpreter's responses to the dreamer's dream are heavily laced with projection. However in dream interpretation there is a corrective not enjoyed by the psychoanalytic interpreter of works of art, the associations of the dreamer. The dreamer's associations guide the psychoanalyst to what is within the dream, and the dialogue purifies as the interpreter more clearly perceives the dreamer's unconscious contents. It must be acknowledged nevertheless that in both there is much room for projective distortion.

THE ANATOMY OF THE ART PIECE

In *The Origins and Psychodynamics of Creativity* (1997), I suggested a structure for the art piece that uses the dream as the model. I suggested that the art piece, like the dream, is a condensed composite of the topical, the personal, and the archetypical.

The *topical* is the general thrust of the purpose and narrative of the art piece. Often the topical is strongly represented in the title or is related to the commission, either the formal commission or the artist's self-assigned and not always fully consciously perceived task. The *personal* reflects the dynamic interaction of the artist's biographical present and past, both conscious and unconscious, with the proposed purpose and task. The *archetypical* repeats the universals integral to human development that find their way into any human endeavor.

An art work can be overly weighted by any of these imperatives. In art if the topical is over weighted, the work is essentially propagandistic; if the personal predominates, the work is idiosyncratic; if the archetypical is over represented, the work is petrified and stereotypical.

---

[7] In the *Moses* study, Freud found he had to return repeatedly to the sculpture to "correct" his evolving ideas.

The art masterpiece, like the dream, is a parsimonious condensation of these conscious/unconscious imperatives operating synergistically without redundancy and ambiguity.

Applying this dream structure to *Hamlet*, topically *Hamlet* is a Renaissance revenge tragedy. Packed in the tragedy are direct and veiled commentaries on the important current socioeconomical and political themes of Elizabethan times—changing views of religion, monarchy, democracy, and society—as medieval England rapidly integrated Renaissance thought marching northward.

On the personal level, it is tempting to follow Freud's (1900) view that Shakespeare wrote *Hamlet* in response to the deaths of his son and father. This personal imperative enlarged the revenge theme, giving the play expanded importance by becoming an exploration of death, responses to death, and issues of continuance.[8] As issues of finiteness emerge, the topical and the personal are immeasurably enhanced by the archetypical—the universally compelling issues of death, transformation, continuance, and finiteness.

Death and the Fear of Finiteness in Hamlet is a study of the multiple meanings packed within the play that account for its capacity to transcend generations, cultures, and epochs. In that sense the book is a study of *Hamlet*'s inconsistencies and ambiguities and a study of "artistic intention."[9] Specifically, the focus of this book is on *Hamlet* as a study of death, transformation, transcendence, and continuance—a study of the fear of finiteness. The book is a study of the play's evocation of the primal call of all of us, *Remember me*.[10]

---

8 It is of interest that in 1900 Freud used the writing of *Hamlet* and its relation to the death of Hamnet in his discussion of mourning as a motivation in creativity. Yet Freud seemed to forget his insightful idea in a letter to Percy Allen in 1935. In that letter, Freud sided with those who felt that the plays could not have been written by Shakespeare and most likely were written by Edward De Vere, the Earl of Oxford.

9 By "artistic intention" I mean that although the artist consciously packs much into a piece, more is placed in the piece than the artist intends or realizes as the artist's unconscious ubiquitously finds its way into the work. "Artistic intention" is the synergistic combination of conscious and unconscious communicating.

10 Lore has it that when King Charles I was facing the executioner's block, he turned to the assembled crowd and said, "Remember me." If this were true, it reminds us of the vast importance of what Shakespeare gives us. He even gave a king his final words.

 Ghost: *Adieu, adieu, adieu, Remember me.* (Act I, Sc. v, line 91)

Man — art, confusion
and art. future
loss, creative
personal denial

2 Cain and Abel

KING HAMLET

A central figure in *Hamlet* is King Hamlet, whose character is revealed through various memories, ghostly appearances, a picture, and Prince Hamlet's hallucination in Act III. These multiple manifestations provide much of the information necessary to understand the complexities of Hamlet's relationship with Fortinbras, Claudius, Gertrude, King Hamlet, and Hamlet himself.

Act I provides several short descriptions of King Hamlet in the first meeting between Hamlet and Horatio.

> **Hamlet:** *But two months dead—nay, not so much, not two—*
> *So excellent a king, that was to this*
> *Hyperion to a satyr, so loving to my mother*
> *That he might not beteem the winds of heaven*
> *Visit her face too roughly....*
>
> ...
>
> **Horatio:** *I saw him once; a was a goodly king.*
> **Hamlet:** *A was a man, take him for all in all:*
> *I shall not look upon his like again.*
>
> ...
>
> **Hamlet:** *His beard was grizzled, no?*
> **Horatio:** *It was as I have seen it in his life,*
> *A sable silver'd.*
>
> (Act I, Sc. ii, lines 138–142; 186–188; 240–242)

But the most vivid "recreation" of King Hamlet occurs in the queen's bed chamber.

> **Hamlet:** *Look here upon this picture, and on this,*
> *The counterfeit presentment of two brothers.*
> *See what a grace was seated on this brow,*
> *Hyperion's curls, the front of Jove himself,*
> *An eye like Mars to threaten and command,*
> *A station like the herald Mercury*
> *New-lighted on a heaven-kissing hill,*
> *A combination and a form indeed*
> *Where every god did seem to set his seal*
> *To give the world assurance of a man.*
> *This was your husband. . . .*
> (Act III, Sc. iv, lines 54–63)

THE GHOST IN ACT I

Medieval theology provides a variety of explanations for why ghosts appear, to whom they appear and to whom they do not, to whom they speak and to whom they do not, and what language must be used to address a ghost (Prosser, 1971; Summers, 1926). In *Hamlet*, an apparition of King Hamlet appears to several characters both major and minor. He appears to Marcellus, Bernardo, Francisco, Horatio, and Hamlet, but he speaks only to Hamlet. The dialogue of the ghost provides much of the archaic reasoning as to why he roams and what he experiences in an afterlife that is all too physically conceived. He affirms the central position that sin, confession, and contrition define one's fate in the afterlife, beliefs that were widely held and practiced in Elizabethan England, although Renaissance influences were beginning to call them into question. These medieval notions, rapidly becoming anachronistic, reprise themselves in the interchange between Laertes and the priest at Ophelia's grave side.

Many *Hamlet* scholars detail inconsistencies in the ghost (Prosser, 1971). Alfred Harbage (1947) notes that George Santayana (1900) describes two ghosts, ". . . a Christian soul in Purgatory, which ought, in theological strictness to be a holy and redeemed soul, a phase of penitential and spiritual experience; . . . (and a) soul (who) fears to scent the morning air, trembles at the cock crow, and instigates the revenging of crime by crime" (p. 103). Commenting on the inconsistencies, Lily Bess Campbell (1930) writes, "If a papist (who believed ghosts to be Christian spirits) and King James (who believed they were demons) and Timothy Bright (who believed they were figments of the brain) had seen the play, as they probably did, each would have gone home confirmed of his own opinion about ghosts" (p. 104). Alfred Harbage (1947) describes three ghosts. He begins with Santayana's description of the ghost as a Christian soul in Purgatory and a second ghost, a fearful soul who instigates revenge. He adds a third that is close to Bright's (1586) and my view, a "third identity . . . apparent when Hamlet can see it and his mother cannot, suggesting that it may be a mere hallucination" (p. 104).

I suggest that the ghost in Act I is a different ghost from the ghost in Act III. I propose that the ghost in Act I is a medieval ghost and the ghost in Act III, an atemporal (psychological) ghost. In short the early ghost reflects the Elizabethan theater tradition that personified popular belief in spirits who return from the grave for varying reasons and purposes. The Act I ghost sets a dramatic effect, a dramatic direction, and within the existing theatrical tradition provides information.[1] In contrast, the ghost in Act III is *the very coinage of* (Hamlet's) *brain* (Act III, Sc. iv, line 139).

THE TASK

In Act I, the ghost delivers a heavy message to Hamlet. He provides convincing indictment of his brother, implies accusations about and prohibits certain actions toward the queen, and makes a direct call for revenge, the nature of which is unspecified although the implication is that Hamlet must kill the king. Save for Claudius, only Hamlet and the audience know the whole story. Because the audience shares the information with Hamlet, it tightly bonds with him in a curiously uncritical way. On this level the play is an uninteresting revenge tragedy.

---

[1] Ghosts continue today only rarely in cinema and in plays. Noel Coward's play *Blithe Spirit* (1941) and the films *Ghost* (1990) and *Topper* (1937) are some examples.

Ghost: *If thou didst ever thy dear father love—*
...
Revenge his foul and most unnatural murder.
(Act I, Sc. v, line 23; 25)

Close evaluation of the task allows for interesting speculation regarding Hamlet's dilemma. These speculations range from Goethe's fully internal, constitutional view that Hamlet is given a task for which by nature he is morally ill equipped,

Ghost: *If thou has nature in thee, bear it not,*
Let not the royal bed of Denmark be
A couch for luxury and damned incest.
(Act I, Sc. v, lines 81–83)

to pragmatic ideas suggesting that Hamlet is given a task that is politically and practically unfeasible.[2]

That external circumstances alone inhibit Hamlet is easily refuted by his mistaken killing of Polonius (an attempt to kill King Claudius who Hamlet believed was hiding behind the arras), the fact that Laertes in response to Polonius's murder threateningly approached the king, and Hamlet's statement

Hamlet: *Sith I have cause, and will, and strength, and means*
To do't....
(Act IV, Sc. iv, lines 45–46)

Clearly, if external circumstance alone prevented Hamlet's action, the play would capture little attention.

REVENGE

Psychoanalytically, revenge is a magical undoing. It is a primitive response of the archaic mind, a mind that continues into maturity largely finding expression only in dreams and fantasies. In revenge, it is as though perpetrating the act on the perpetrator of the act undoes

---

[2] Goethe's ideas echo the ghost's words, *If thou hast nature in thee*. With this as basis, Freud (1900) evolves a more subtle understanding of unconscious conflicts and conscience that posits why Hamlet delays in revenge.
    Hamlet: *Thus conscience does make cowards of us all,*
    (Act III, Sc. i, line 83)

the act. To avenge a murder "an eye for an eye" requires death of the murderer. Psychically, such as in the dream or the child's wish, the loss is eradicated by the elimination of the perpetrator of the loss. It is *lex talionis*, the primitive golden rule.

The psychoanalytic structural view of revenge as an archaic magical undoing contrasts with Eleanor Prosser's (1971) phenomenological and global view of revenge. As she writes, "All men hunger for revenge . . . the defiant refusal to submit to injury, the desire to assert one's identity by retaliation, their gnawing ache to assault injustice by giving measure for measure" (p. 253). Although Prosser's study of *Hamlet* is an invaluable resource, it suffers from a lack of multilayered, dynamic, developmental understanding. The strength and the weakness of her work is her tendency, thoughtfully so, to be phenomenological without inferring unconscious motivations and meanings.

The simplicity of revenge is appealingly deceptive. Evaluating Hamlet's *means* puts his dilemma in broad relief. The Prayer Scene amply demonstrates that Hamlet has easy opportunities to kill Claudius. Hamlet has the *means* in the simple sense. Left open is the question of the nature of the revenge available to Hamlet. Could Hamlet's revenge be complete without full exposure of Claudius?

A retaliatory murder of Claudius meets the criteria for personal revenge and fulfills the *commandment* of the ghost.[3] Yet, Hamlet's murdering an unexposed Claudius ironically would ensure Claudius an honored place in history and result in Hamlet's being branded with regicide. Claudius would be made heroic and Hamlet destroyed. The true and full story could never be told and the destruction of Hamlet, King Hamlet's only heir, leaves King Hamlet without continuance.

Adding to Hamlet's dilemma is the powerful admonition of the ghost,

> **Ghost:** *But howsomever thou pursuest this act,*

---

[3] *Commandment* is Hamlet's word.
   Hamlet: *And thy commandment all alone shall live*
   Within the book and volume of my brain,
   (Act. I, Sc. v, lines 102–103)

> *Taint not thy mind nor let thy soul contrive*
> *Against thy mother aught. Leave her to heaven,*
> (Act I, Sc. v, lines 84–86)

Without question, for Hamlet *howsomever* becomes a big word and the requirement of *taint not thy mind* a tall order.

In short, Claudius's murder, though immediate and magically powerful, ultimately would be meaningless. With it, everyone loses. Fearing the futility of revenge, Hamlet's requesting and being moved to tears by the player who recites the events in the life of Pyrrhus at Troy seems all too understandable.

The multiple ironies involved in evaluating the *means* are enacted on a Catholic level in the Prayer Scene. If Hamlet were to kill Claudius in a state of grace, Claudius's spiritual immortalization would be ensured and both King Hamlet and Hamlet would suffer eternally in Purgatory and worse (Prosser, 1971).

> **Hamlet:** *Now might I do it pat, now a is a-praying.*
> *And now I'll do't.*
>   *And so a goes to heaven;*
> *And so am I reveng'd. That would be scann'd:*
> *A villain kills my father, and for that*
> *I, his sole son, do this same villain send*
> *To heaven.*
> (Act. III, Sc. iii, lines 73–78)

Yet psychoanalytically, Hamlet's thinking that the king is in the act of contrition is a flimsy rationalization for delay. Ever vigilant for the opportunity for irony, Shakespeare lets us know that the king is incapable of contrition.

> **King:** *My words fly up, my thoughts remain below.*
> *Words without thoughts never to heaven go.*
> (Act III, Sc. iii, lines 97–98)

Largely unaddressed by Hamlet's critics is whether he at any time has the *means* for revenge in the full sense? Rarely asked is the question: does Hamlet have the *means* to expose Claudius (and perhaps

Gertrude)? In fact, Claudius ironically dies with his incest and regicide never exposed.

CLAUDIUS

The question of Claudius's guilt preoccupies only Hamlet. The queen, perhaps an accomplice, is unquestioning, and the court as a whole seems glad to accept the story of King Hamlet's death. In the play Shakespeare does not clarify who invents the story. The likelihood is that Claudius is the author. If that is so, then his inventing the story of death by a serpent is unconsciously self-revealing and may be our first glimpse into Claudius's conflicted, unconscious self-loathing, a self-loathing heavily mixed with guilt. Even Polonius's mild comment mid-play, a comment to Ophelia,

> **Polonius:** . . . —*We are oft to blame in this,*
> *'Tis too much prov'd, that with devotion's visage*
> *And pious action we do sugar o'er*
> *The devil himself.*
> (Act III, Sc. i, lines 46–49)

provokes this aside,

> **King:** *O, 'tis too true.*
> *How smart a lash that speech doth give my conscience.*
> *The harlot's cheek, beautied with plast'ring art,*
> *Is not more ugly to the thing that helps it*
> *Than is my deed to my most painted word.*
> *O heavy burden!*
> (Act III, Sc. i, lines 49–54)

Later we hear,

> **King:** *O, my offence is rank, it smells to heaven;*
> (Act III, Sc. iii, line 36)

The Prayer Scene, scarcely sixty lines long, is a deep look into Claudius's interior (Prosser, 1971). It is a dialogue with himself, not with God.

> **King:** ... —*but O, what form of prayer*
> *Can serve my turn? 'Forgive me my foul murder?'*
> *That cannot be, since I am still possess'd*
> *Of those effects for which I did the murder—*
> (Act III, Sc. iii, lines 51–54)

Claudius's attempt to assuage his guilt through contrition is a failure. He knows that he cannot attain grace and retain the rewards gained by the sinful act. In the existential tradition, not so stated, Claudius knows that in the end one must come to grips with one's actions.

> **King:** *There is no shuffling, there the action lies*
> *In his true nature, and we ourselves compell'd*
> *Even to the teeth and forehead of our faults*
> *To give in evidence. . . .*
> (Act III, Sc. iii, lines 61–64)

Claudius knows that one cannot escape oneself. His tormented self-search ends in a plea for help in overcoming his pride and finding inner peace.

> **King:** ... *Help, angels! Make assay.*
> *Bow, stubborn knees; and heart with strings of steel,*
> *Be soft as sinews of the new-born babe.*
> *All may be well.*
> (Act III, Sc. iii, lines 69–72)

The passage is strikingly free of any evocation of God as a personification or a dispenser of mercy and salvation. It is best understood as a man who knows that he must come to terms with himself and what he has done and who knows that he cannot.

Despite his lack of compunction in achieving self-serving goals, Claudius is not an amoral psychopath. Surprisingly, he fully understands that ultimate justice overshadows day-to-day pragmatism.

> **King:** *In the corrupted currents of this world*
> *Offence's gilded hand may shove by justice,*
> *And oft 'tis seen the wicked prize itself*
> *Buys out the law. But 'tis not so above:*
> (Act III, Sc. iii, lines 57–60)

Claudius reveals much about himself later in a discourse with Laertes when he details his distrust of love and relationships.

> **King:** *Not that I think you did not love your father,*
> *But that I know love is begun by time,*
> *And that I see, in passages of proof,*
> *Time qualifies the spark and fire of it.*
> *There lives within the very flame of love*
> *A kind of wick or snuff that will abate it;*
> *And nothing is at a like goodness still,*
> *For goodness, growing to a pleurisy,*
> *Dies in his own too-much. That we would do,*
> *We should do when we would: for this 'would' changes*
> *And hath abatements and delays as many*
> *As there are tongues, are hands, are accidents,*
> *And then this 'should' is like a spendthrift's sigh*
> *That hurts by easing....*
> (Act IV, Sc. vii, lines 109–122)

THE PLOT TO KILL HAMLET

As the momentum of events gathers, Claudius's evilness inevitably multiplies and the scope ever widens. His earlier self-loathing is replaced by a monumental ability for self-preservation. When he hears that Hamlet has slain Polonius, Claudius has no question as to Hamlet's intention nor what must be done.

> **King:** *O heavy deed!*
> *It had been so with us had we been there.*
> *His liberty is full of threats to all—*
> *To you yourself, to us, to everyone.*
> (Act IV, Sc. i, lines 12–15)

In his plot to kill the banished Hamlet we see Claudius's sense of self-preservation and amoral pragmatism in full cry. In contrast to the torment and conflict that characterized the Prayer Scene, once Claudius has ascertained that Hamlet is a threat to him, even without knowledge that Hamlet knows his secret, Claudius plans Hamlet's elimination. It is not revenge; it is survival. He plans murder to eliminate rather than to retaliate. In keeping with his deviousness, others are to do the killing.

> **King:** *I like him not, nor stands it safe with us*
> *To let his madness range. Therefore prepare you.*
> *I your commission will forthwith dispatch,*
> *And he to England shall along with you.*
> (Act III, Sc. iii, lines 1–4)

When the first attempt to have Hamlet murdered is foiled, Claudius's second attempt fully evidences his capacity to prey on weakness and to manipulate the unsuspecting. One cannot help but wonder if his manipulating of Laertes does not provide a look at how he played upon Gertrude's weaknesses before murdering King Hamlet.

Laertes, filled with the desire to avenge his father's murder, returns to Elsinore and confronts Claudius, who with remarkable cunning turns Laertes to his side.

> **King:** *. . . he which hath your noble father slain*
> *Pursu'd my life.*
> (Act IV, Sc. vii, lines 4–5)

Increasing his anguish, Laertes finds his sister *driven into desp'rate terms* (Act IV, Sc. vii, line 26), an anguish almost unbearably intensified by her subsequent tragic death.

While engaged with Laertes, Claudius receives a letter from Hamlet.[4] He is astonished to learn that Hamlet has survived the plot to kill him in England. Claudius immediately enlists the unwary Laertes to his cause against Hamlet.

> **Laertes:** *It warms the very sickness in my heart*
> *That I shall live and tell him to his teeth,*
> *'Thus diest thou'.*

---

[4] Horatio, who has remained at the castle, receives a letter from Hamlet telling him that pirates had overtaken the ship bearing him to England. Hamlet writes that even though he was taken prisoner, he was treated well and offered escape, and he has now returned to Denmark. He asks Horatio to make sure that the letters he has written to his mother and to Claudius, borne by the messenger, are delivered. Claudius reads out loud from the letter from Hamlet. We are never to know the contents of the letter to his mother.

> **King:**   *If it be so, Laertes—*
> *As how should it be so, how otherwise?—*
> *Will you be rul'd by me?*
> (Act IV, Sc. vii, lines 54–58)

Claudius skillfully plays on the easily malleable, immature Laertes, and he hatches a second plot to kill Hamlet. Laertes literally is his foil.

> **King:** *. . . I will work him*
> *To an exploit, now ripe in my device,*
> *Under the which he shall not choose but fall;*
> *And for his death no wind of blame shall breathe,*
> *But even his mother shall uncharge the practice*
> *And call it accident.*
> **Laertes:**   *My lord, I will be rul'd,*
> *The rather if you could devise it so*
> *That I might be the organ.*
> . . .
> **King:** *Laertes, was your father dear to you?*
> *Or are you like the painting of a sorrow,*
> *A face without a heart?*
> (Act IV, Sc. vii, lines 62–69; 106–108)

Claudius maneuvers a startling challenge.

> **King:** *Hamlet comes back; what would you undertake*
> *To show yourself in deed your father's son*
> *More than in words?*
> (Act IV, Sc. vii, lines 123–124)

Without hesitation, Laertes answers,

> **Laertes:**   *To cut his throat i'th' church.*
> (Act IV, Sc. vii, line 125)

A pleased Claudius responds,

> **King:** *Revenge should have no bounds. . . .*
> (Act IV, Sc. vii, line 127)

Once assured that Laertes is on his side, Claudius advances the scheme that will result in the climax of the play.

THE END OF CLAUDIUS

At the play's end, Hamlet mortally wounds Claudius with the sword poisoned by Laertes that has lethally poisoned Laertes and Hamlet. Hamlet then forces Claudius to drink the poisoned wine Claudius intended for Hamlet, the same wine that poisoned Gertrude. Claudius's agonal words are strikingly free of religious call or plea. Futilely he cries out.

> **King:** *O yet defend me, friends. I am but hurt.*
> (Act V, Sc. ii, line 329)

His death is a death with resignation. There is no evidence of fear of finiteness or wish for continuance.[5]

Hamlet's terse statement

> **Hamlet:** *Follow my mother.*
> (Act V, Sc. ii, line 332)

seems a strange farewell to Claudius in that he hated their union. In this scene of ultimate farewells, poignantly Hamlet cannot forgive his mother. *Wretched Queen, adieu* (Act V, Sc. ii, line 338) is the best he can do.[6]

CAIN AND ABEL

Both Claudius and King Hamlet seek revenge through someone else. In each case it is an older man acting through a young man, each bringing about the death of the young man. The first-born son is sacrificed. The Sacrifice of Isaac, the Passover, the Flight into Egypt,

---

5 From the beginning, Hamlet refused to be Claudius's "son" and heir apparent.
>   **King:** *... We pray you throw to earth*
>   *This unprevailing woe, and think of us*
>   *As of a father; for let the world take note*
>   *You are the most immediate to our throne,*
>   *And with no less nobility of love*
>   *Than that which dearest father bears his son*
>   *Do I impart toward you. ...*
>   (Act I, Sc. ii, lines 106–112)

6 Even bearing in mind that the Elizabethan meaning of "wretched" was closer to *pitiable* than its modern pejorative meaning, this is a cool and detached good-bye.

and the Crucifixion are evoked as ominous archetypal underpinning to the play.

The Claudius–King Hamlet interchange is more than regicide with all its implications of father (king representing the father) murder. Claudius's envy of King Hamlet is clear. Through his brother's murder, Claudius with a single act gains both queen and crown.

> **King:** . . . *since I am still possess'd*
> *Of those effects for which I did the murder—*
> *My crown, mine own ambition, and my queen.*
> (Act III, Sc. iii, lines 53–55)

His murder of King Hamlet recreates the first murder. Cain slew Abel in an angry fit of jealousy. The Claudius–King Hamlet murder is primal sibling rivalry.

> **King:** *It hath the primal eldest curse upon't—*
> *A brother's murder. . . .*
> (Act III, Sc. iii, lines 37–38)

Through the Cain–Abel theme, the royal family of Denmark transforms into the primal family. The first mortals, the first to have to deal with death, populate the stage. Revealed is that the play revolves around humankind's confrontation with finiteness.

3 | Gertrude: Queen, Wife, and Mother

Probably the most elusive character in *Hamlet* is Queen Gertrude. Seen as complex and scheming or simple and shallow, it is difficult to ascertain her position as wife and mother prior to or after the death of King Hamlet. Her supporters and her detractors are sharply divided regarding her relationship with Hamlet, the role she played in King Hamlet's death, her relationship with Claudius prior to King Hamlet's death, and her *o'er-hasty marriage* (Eissler, 1971; Wilson, 1970). In general, critics through the centuries have not treated her kindly.

Deeply immersed in court intrigue, she remains an enigma. Although her dependency on Claudius is apparent, careful reading of her lines shows scant evidence of affection for the king. Nevertheless, Claudius remains consistently deferential and fawning with her.[1]

> **King:** *... and for myself—*
> *My virtue or my plague, be it either which—*
> *She is so conjunctive to my life and soul*
> *That, as the star moves not but in his sphere,*
> *I could not but by her. ...*
> (Act IV, Sc. vii, lines 12–16)

In contrast, Gertrude's involvement with Hamlet is intense. Whether the relationship with him is a selfish or authentic love, it is widely held that mother and son are deeply intertwined. Yet, the depth of Gertrude's engrossment is largely based on one line:

> **King:** *... The Queen his mother*

---

[1] Although Gertrude is frequently played as coquettish with and fawning over Claudius, perusal of the lines does not require such an interpretation.

Lives almost by his looks, ...
(Act IV, Sc. vii, lines 11–12)

Save for Hamlet and Horatio, no one publicly or privately questions or criticizes Gertrude's behavior, past and present.

Horatio: *My lord, I came to see your father's funeral.*
Hamlet: *I prithee do not mock me, fellow-student.*
I think it was to see my mother's wedding.
Horatio: *Indeed, my lord, it follow'd hard upon.*
(Act I, Sc. ii, lines 176–179)

SEEMS AND SEEMING

As psychoanalysis broadened its scope beyond the study of the origin and psychodynamics of mental symptoms, it began to study the psychodynamics of character formation and character functioning. As part of this broadened interest, Helene Deutsch (1942) described a kind of character disturbance she called the *as if personality* in which the individual is what s/he thinks s/he is expected to be. Reflecting a poorly integrated protean sense of self, the individual becomes *as if* s/he is rather than as s/he is. The *as if personality* cannot (as Hamlet longed to) *be or not to be*, it can only be what it thinks it is expected to be. Viewing Gertrude as an *as if* makes her less superficial and more pitiful.

Hamlet early in the play confronts Gertrude with this *as if* quality.

Queen: *Good Hamlet, cast thy nighted colour off,*
And let thine eye look like a friend on Denmark.
Do not for ever with thy vailed lids
Seek for thy noble father in the dust.
Thou know'st 'tis common: all that lives must die,
Passing through nature to eternity.
Hamlet: *Ay, madam, it is common.*
Queen: *If it be,*
Why seems it so particular with thee?
Hamlet: *Seems, madam? Nay, it is. I know not 'seems'.*
(Act I, Sc. ii, lines 68–76)

Hamlet continues his subtle berating of the queen. He reminds her that it is not a matter of appearance nor tears that count but that of feelings and actions.

> **Hamlet:** ... *These indeed seem,*
> *For they are actions that a man might play;*
> (Act I, Sc. ii, lines 83–84)

King Hamlet tellingly also uses the word *seeming* when he talks about Gertrude.

> **Ghost:** *The will of my most seeming-virtuous queen.*
> (Act I, Sc. v, line 46)

Hamlet's confrontation with the queen is repeated in high drama in the Closet Scene.

> **Hamlet:** *Come, come, and sit you down, you shall not budge.*
> *You go not till I set you up a glass*
> *Where you may see the inmost part of you.*
> (Act III, Sc. iv, lines 17–19)

Early in the play, Gertrude emerges as a highly ambivalent, dependent, guilt-ridden woman who desperately moves from one powerful man to another. From this view, the idea that she was an accomplice in the plot to kill King Hamlet fades. She seems more a woman who clings to anyone who can provide her with power and protection, a view suggested by the ghost.

> **Ghost:** *With witchcraft of his wit, with traitorous gifts—*
> *O wicked wit, and gifts that have the power*
> *So to seduce!—won to his shameful lust*
> *The will of my most seeming-virtuous queen.*
> (Act I, Sc. v, lines 43–46)

The ghost does not go so far as to accuse Gertrude directly of being an accomplice in the murder, but he falls only slightly short of it. Even though the ghost is tangential in his accusations regarding her role in his murder, he is clear in his accusation of her infidelity.

Gertrude's protean self does not preclude an ability to be insightful, as we see in her sharp dismissal of Polonius's theory regarding Hamlet's illness.

> **King:** *He tells me, my dear Gertrude, he hath found*
> *The head and source of all your son's distemper.*
> **Queen:** *I doubt it is no other but the main,*
> *His father's death and our o'er-hasty marriage.*
> (Act II, Sc. ii, lines 54–57)

To see Gertrude as easily manipulated and dependent does not mean that she is without manipulative ability.

> **Queen** (to Rosencrantz and Guildenstern):
> *Good gentlemen, he hath much talk'd of you,*
> *And sure I am, two men there is not living*
> *To whom he more adheres. If it will please you*
> *To show us so much gentry and good will*
> *As to expend your time with us awhile*
> *For the supply and profit of our hope,*
> *Your visitation shall receive such thanks*
> *As fits a king's remembrance.*
> (Act II, Sc. ii, lines 19–26)

More telling is her silence when Polonius and Claudius plan to use Ophelia to deceive Hamlet while they secretly look on. The king's response to Polonius's plan is simple.

> **King:**   *We will try it.*
> (Act II, Sc. ii, line 67)

Gertrude remains silent, allowing it to happen. When the plan is presented to Ophelia and the king asks Gertrude to leave them as Hamlet approaches, she responds in tacit complicity.

> **Gertrude:**   *I shall obey you.*
> (Act III, Sc. i, line 37)

GERTRUDE AND HAMLET

Freud (1897–1902, 1900) used Hamlet's relationship with his mother in his exposition of the Oedipus complex. Freud's study is of Hamlet and his inability to pursue the ghost's charge. In this work, Freud tells us little of Gertrude herself.

A careful study of her lines reveals reticence in her feelings toward Hamlet. Her first words to Hamlet are a request that he become friends with her new husband.

> **Queen:** *Good Hamlet, cast thy nighted colour off,*
> *And let thine eye look like a friend on Denmark.*
> (Act I, Sc. ii, lines 68–69)

She then requests that Hamlet remain in Elsinore Castle and not return to school. Although seemingly loving and caring, her request is essentially self-serving.

> **Queen:** *Let not thy mother lose her prayers, Hamlet.*
> *I pray thee stay with us, go not to Wittenberg.*
> (Act I, Sc. ii, lines 118–119)

There is no other direct interaction between Hamlet and his mother until Act III. During the play within the play, she enticingly says

> **Queen:** *Come hither, my dear Hamlet, sit by me.*
> (Act III, Sc. ii, line 107)

Yet as the scene heats up, her response quickly cools with his provocative questioning.

> **Queen:** *The lady doth protest too much, methinks.*
> (Act III, Sc. ii, line 225)

These lines are the totality of direct conversations between Gertrude and Hamlet until the Closet Scene.

THE CLOSET SCENE

As the scene opens, Gertrude is more concerned about Hamlet's treatment of Claudius than about Hamlet himself. Her overarching concern is her, perhaps their, relationship with the king. Her concern is unwarranted in that for political reasons and his desire for Gertrude, Claudius is intensely interested in maintaining a good relationship with Hamlet.

> **King:**   *O, for two special reasons,*
> *Which may to you perhaps seem much unsinew'd,*
> *But yet to me th'are strong. The Queen his mother*
> *Lives almost by his looks, and for myself—*
> *My virtue or my plague, be it either which—*
> *She is so conjunctive to my life and soul*
> *That, as the star moves not but in his sphere,*
> *I could not but by her. The other motive*
> *Why to a public count I might not go*
> *Is the great love the general gender bear him,*
> (Act IV, Sc. vii, lines 9–18)

As the rapid stichomythia between Hamlet and Gertrude develops, the interaction becomes vitriolic.

> **Queen:** *Hamlet, thou hast thy father much offended.*
> **Hamlet:** *Mother, you have my father much offended.*
> **Queen:** *Come, come, you answer with an idle tongue.*
> **Hamlet:** *Go, go, you question with a wicked tongue.*
> **Queen:** (seeming to soften[2]) *Why, how now, Hamlet?*
> **Hamlet:** (seeming incredulous that she should ask[3])
>   *What's the matter now?*
> **Queen:** *Have you forgot me?*
> (Act III, Sc. iv, lines 8–13)

Hamlet's reply is perhaps the most searing filial denunciation of a mother in literature.

> **Hamlet:**   *No, by the rood, not so.*
> *You are the Queen, your husband's brother's wife,*
> *And, would it were not so, you are my mother.*
> (Act III, Sc. iv, lines 13–15)

---

[2] Author's comment.
[3] Author's comment.

It is at once a denunciation and a total renunciating obliteration of her and of himself.

The confrontation continues. Her initial response is to fear for her life.

> **Queen:** *What wilt thou do? Thou wilt not murder me?*
> *Help, ho!*
> (Act III, Sc. iv, lines 20–21)

The interaction changes suddenly as Polonius, alarmed, calls out from behind the arras. Thinking that it is Claudius, Hamlet stabs through the curtain. The queen recoils in horror. Without pausing, Hamlet directly confronts Gertrude with her complicity in the murder of his father.

> **Hamlet:** *A bloody deed. Almost as bad, good mother,*
> *As kill a king and marry with his brother.*
> (Act III, Sc. iv, lines 28–29)

The question of her complicity may rest on the interpretation of her response:

> **Queen:** *As kill a king?*
> (Act III, Sc. iv, line 30)

Whether her question is true puzzlement or fending off the accusation, Hamlet is steadfast in his belief.

> **Hamlet:** *Ay, lady, it was my word.—*
> (Act III, Sc. iv, line 30)

At this point, Hamlet pulls back the arras and discovers the slain Polonius. Without remorse he continues his unrelenting confrontation with Gertrude.

> **Hamlet:** *And let me wring your heart; for so I shall*
> *If it be made of penetrable stuff,*
> *If damned custom have not braz'd it so,*
> *That it be proof and bulwark against sense.*
> (Act III, Sc. iv, lines 35–38)

The excoriation becomes progressively and literally sexualized.

Hamlet: *Nay, but to live
In the rank sweat of an enseamed bed,
Stew'd in corruption, honeying and making love
Over the nasty sty!*
(Act III, Sc. iv, lines 91–94)

Gertrude pleads,

Gertrude: *O speak to me no more.
These words like daggers enter in my ears.
No more, sweet Hamlet.*
(Act III, Sc. iv, lines 94–96)

Although suffering as Hamlet challenges the very bond of their relationship and the core of her self, she evidences no sign of repentance or confession. *Sweet* is the warmest word Gertrude ever uses with Hamlet.[4]

As the sexualized intensity in the interchange increases, the interaction is abruptly changed when Hamlet hallucinates the ghost. By introducing a third, the father, the hallucination literally separates

---

4 Twice in the play she addresses him as *dear*. In the play within the play she calls to him,
    Queen: *Come hither, my dear Hamlet, sit by me.*
    (Act III, Sc. ii, line 107)
and as she dies,
    Queen: *... O my dear Hamlet!
    The drink, the drink! I am poison'd.*
    (Act V, Sc. ii, lines 315–316)
We get some insight into Gertrude as a mother in the scene in which Polonius proposes to Claudius that they spy on Hamlet and Ophelia. Gertrude readily and unquestioningly accepts the idea of spying on one's children.
   It is also of interest in evaluating the relationships of Hamlet to his parents that on the first meeting between the ghost and Hamlet, in revealing the facts of his murder, King Hamlet laments his loss.
    Ghost: *Thus was I, sleeping, by a brother's hand
    Of life, of crown, of queen at once dispatch'd,*
    (Act I, Sc. v, lines 74–75)
There is no mention of the loss of his son.
   Re-creating a childhood for a character in a play is an exercise in conjecture, for characters in plays only have childhoods to the extent that the playwright gives them one. Yet however intense the Hamlet–Gertrude relationship may be, it is tempting to think about the scant number of affectionate moments Gertrude shows her son. Her affective limitation coupled with the lack of affectionate response from the ghost–father suggests barrenness in Hamlet's relationship with his parents, a barrenness that stands in marked contrast to the fully loving remembrances he has of his relationship with Yorick (Act V, Sc. i, lines 178–189).

the mother–son dyad. To protect him from acting on his intense sexual and hostile impulses toward his mother, Hamlet's tormented mind conjures (hallucinates) the father. In psychosis, Hamlet re-creates the Oedipal triangle.

> **Ghost:** *O step between her and her fighting soul.*
> *Conceit in weakest bodies strongest works.*
> *Speak to her, Hamlet.*
> (Act III, Sc. iv, lines 113–115)

Gertrude now fully recognizes Hamlet's psychotic state.

> **Queen:** *Alas, he's mad.*
> (Act III, Sc. iv, line 106)

Her awareness of Hamlet's deranged mind undermines the fragile hold he has on himself, and Hamlet frantically attempts to reassure Gertrude in order to reassure himself.

> **Hamlet:** . . . *It is not madness*
> *That I have utter'd. . .*
> *. . . Mother, for love of grace,*
> *Lay not that flattering unction to your soul,*
> *That not your trespass but my madness speaks.*
> (Act III, Sc. iv, lines 143–144; 146–148)

As he continues his diatribe, the intensity increases with the sexual imagery becoming more patent. It is as though he is in bed with Gertrude and Claudius.

> **Hamlet:** . . . *But go not to my uncle's bed.*
> *Assume a virtue, if you have it not.*
> . . .
> *Not this, by no means, that I bid you do:*
> *Let the bloat King tempt you again to bed,*
> *Pinch wanton on your cheek, call you his mouse,*
> *And let him, for a pair of reechy kisses,*
> *Or paddling in your neck with his damn'd fingers,*
> *Make you to ravel all this matter out*
> (Act III, Sc. iv, lines 161–162; 183–188)

Gertrude makes a solemn promise not to tell what has happened.

Queen: *Be thou assur'd, if words be made of breath,*
And breath of life, I have no life to breathe
What thou hast said to me.
(Act III, Sc. iv, lines 199–201)

With utter crassness and curious couplets that monstrously refer to his misdeed, Hamlet exits carrying the dead Polonius. He gives his mother graphic evidence of what he has become, showing her what she has done to him.

Hamlet: *This man shall set me packing.*
I'll lug the guts into the neighbour room.
Mother, good night indeed. This counsellor
Is now most still, most secret, and most grave,
Who was in life a foolish prating knave.
Come, sir, to draw toward an end with you.
Good night, mother.
(Act III, Sc. iv, lines 213–219)

QUEEN OF GRIEF AND MISERY

As Hamlet exits with Polonius, Claudius enters. Even though she has solemnly promised Hamlet to keep secret all that transpired, a visibly upset Gertrude tells the king of the extent of Hamlet's mental derangement and the senseless death of Polonius. However, in a rare instance of actively protecting her son, Gertrude does not tell Claudius that Hamlet intimated that they were King Hamlet's murderers. Claudius immediately and accurately senses that the queen and he are in great danger.

King: *O heavy deed!*
It had been so with us had we been there.
His liberty is full of threats to all—
To you yourself, to us, to everyone.
(Act IV, Sc. i, lines 12–15)

We do not hear from Gertrude again until her appearance with Horatio and a gentleman who implore her to talk to the now distraught Ophelia. Although reluctant,

> **Queen:** *I will not speak with her.*
> (Act IV, Sc. v, line 1)

she is persuaded by Horatio, who uncharacteristically is more concerned about the trouble Ophelia may cause than about Ophelia, a major departure toward pragmatism.

> **Horatio:** *'Twere good she were spoken with, for she may strew*
> *Dangerous conjectures in ill-breeding minds.*
> (Act IV, Sc. v, lines 14–15)

Perhaps Horatio is revealing an emerging cynical corruptibility. Is he becoming like the Court?

Gertrude agrees to talk to Ophelia. When alone, in an important self-search, she professes her guilt, although she does not make clear for what she is guilty. Forlornly she recognizes that she is in a downward spiral of grief and misery that involve all at Elsinore.

> **Queen:** *(aside) To my sick soul, as sin's true nature is,*
> *Each toy seems prologue to some great amiss.*
> *So full of artless jealousy is guilt,*
> *It spills itself in fearing to be spilt.*
> (Act IV, Sc. v, lines 17–20)

Gertrude tries to quiet Ophelia when the king appears. Claudius attempts to sooth the girl, but to no avail. It is not until Gertrude has to inform the returned enraged Laertes of Ophelia's death that we next hear from the queen. Although filled with sadness, she shows little sympathy.

> **Queen:** *One woe doth tread upon another's heel,*
> (Act IV, Sc. vii, line 162)

It is only at Ophelia's burial that we hear truly tender and caring words from Gertrude. In the depths of tragedy, she reveals an ability to feel and to be.

> **Queen:** *(scattering flowers)* *Sweets to the sweet. Farewell.*
> *I hop'd thou shouldst have been my Hamlet's wife:*
> *I thought thy bride-bed to have deck'd, sweet maid,*
> *And not have strew'd thy grave.*
> (Act V, Sc. i, lines 236–239)

Later, in the confrontation between Laertes and Hamlet, she seems changed. She demonstrates compassion and motherly protection for her son.

> **Queen:** *For love of God forbear him.*
> …
> *And thus awhile the fit will work on him.*
> *Anon, as patient as the female dove*
> *When that her golden couplets are disclos'd,*
> *His silence will sit drooping.*
> (Act V, Sc. i, line 268; lines 280–283)

Gertrude gains importance in the complex Duel Scene. There is always the question as to why Hamlet agrees to the duel; even more puzzling is Gertrude's endorsement of it. It seems another instance of her siding with those in power. Yet during this complex scene, she remains steadfastly on Hamlet's side.

> **Queen:** *He's fat and scant of breath.*
> *Here, Hamlet, take my napkin, rub thy brows.*
> *The Queen carouses to thy fortune, Hamlet.*
> (Act V, Sc. ii, lines 290–292)

As Gertrude realizes that she is poisoned and that the king had intended to kill Hamlet, she cries out,

> **Queen:** *No, no, the drink, the drink! O my dear Hamlet!*
> *The drink, the drink! I am poison'd.*
> (Act V, Sc. ii, lines 315–316)

In her agonal scene, she attempts to reach out to Hamlet, yet her last words are concern for herself.

THE END OF GERTRUDE

Torn by guilt, at best, Gertrude seems driven by dependency. Desperately she tries to hang on to her son and second husband. She is a mother who vainly attempts to reconcile her son with his loathed stepfather largely to assure her situation and ease her conscience. There is scant evidence of love for either husband; largely we hear about clinging and dependency. With her son, although intense, the relationship is emotionally barren.

Yet during the course of the play, some change in Gertrude emerges. The Closet Scene is pivotal. She is brought to see what she has done. Most poignantly, she is brought to see that she has destroyed her son. Through an unrelenting cascade of tragedy, she comes to acknowledge her guilt. She begins to feel and to be.

Over the years, there have been many Gertrudes, but largely on stage and in the literature she remains protean. It must be concluded that we only catch glimpses into her personality. In fact she appears in many scenes but has few lines. Although strongly drawn, she is a vacuous creature. Sadly, she *seems* to be more than she is. She gives us no clear idea of what she thinks about life or death. As she fatalistically proclaimed, *all that lives must die* (Act I, Sc. ii, line 72), her end is inevitable. She vanishes into death.

4 | Laertes, Horatio, Fortinbras, and Hamlet

LAERTES AND REVENGE

Laertes personifies revenge in its baldest form. All arguments to rationalize Hamlet's delay of vengeance fade when Laertes marches into the palace and threatens the king.[1] Laertes' father has been killed. Without evidence, thought, or perspective, Laertes seeks to kill his father's killer.

Laertes is filled with omnipotence and without sense of vulnerability. His approach to life is simple. In his advice to Ophelia before departing for France, Laertes shows obvious caring. He is clear in his advice, yet he easily absolves himself from the very temptations about which he warns his sister.

Like an adolescent, Laertes has strong emotions and an impulsive quality.[2] His devotion to his father and his sister is profound. In an adolescent way he is dutiful and playfully depreciating of his father. When confronted with his father's murder, he becomes singular in purpose, directly threatening the life of the king.

The strength of Laertes' emotions and his unconflicted, unquestioning sense of right and wrong allow him to be led easily and unwittingly. He is an easy foil for Claudius's unscrupulous manipulation. As with any adolescent, the fear of finiteness is not an issue. His sole interest is the elimination of the perpetrator of the wrong. Without knowing it, while revengefully preparing a grave for Hamlet, he prepares a grave for himself.

---

1 Arguments for Hamlet's hesitation include that the king is closely guarded, that Hamlet risks an uprising of the people were the king attacked, and that any assault on the king would be Hamlet's asking for death.
2 Laertes' age is unclear. Like Hamlet, he is a student and is about to return to university. Laertes seems a somewhat over-aged adolescent.

In their final confrontation, Hamlet's confession of madness and Hamlet's apologies have no meaning for Laertes. He is blinded by and singular in his quest for revenge. It is only when he realizes that he is about to die that he reassesses what has happened. Without hesitation, his last gasps are attempts to make things right. He bluntly accuses.

> **Laertes:** . . . *The King—the King's to blame.*
> (Act V, Sc. ii, line 326)

The forgiveness he beseeches is not divine but rather that of worldly Hamlet. He pleads for Hamlet's forgiveness.

> **Laertes:** *Exchange forgiveness with me, noble Hamlet.*
> *Mine and my father's death come not upon thee,*
> *Nor thine on me.*
> (Act V, Sc. ii, lines 334–336)

Laertes maintains the audience's interest and affection because of his youthful exuberance. Eventually, he earns our sympathy because of his simple, unapologetic forthrightness.

> **Laertes:** *Why, as a woodcock to mine own springe, Osric.*
> *I am justly kill'd with mine own treachery.*
> (Act V, Sc. ii, lines 312–313)

He is the antipathy of Hamlet and Horatio. Laertes begins the play as an exuberant optimist and ends as a tragic young man who has been duped by an evil manipulator. He personifies the futility of revenge. His simple reactions are doomed to failure. Ironically, like King Hamlet's family, Polonius's family also becomes extinct.

HORATIO AND HAMLET

For many, Horatio is the most admirable character in the play. The steadfastness of his loyalty to Hamlet, perhaps a mature version of the beautiful, aim-inhibited homosexual love of Romeo and Mercutio, is inspiring.[3]

---

[3] Psychoanalysis differentiates between *latent* and *aim-inhibited* homosexuality. *Latent* or *repressed homosexuality* is frequently manifested by reaction formation homophobia, which is fear of and hatred toward homosexuality. *Aim-inhibited homosexuality* is a nonphysical erotic love between same-sex individuals. In the male, *aim-inhibited homosexuality* is found in loving friendships and in teacher–student, coach–athlete, mentor–mentored, and most clearly in father–son relationships. It is fully loving without physical erotic manifestations.

LAERTES, HORATIO, FORTINBRAS, AND HAMLET

Like Hamlet, Horatio is an introspective, philosophical young man. Although often seen as the personification of Renaissance humanism, careful reading of his lines reveals that he, like Hamlet, frequently waivers between the "new" way of thinking and archaic constructs. At the death of Hamlet he utters

> **Horatio:** *I am more an antique Roman than a Dane.*
> (Act V, Sc. ii, line 346)

and lunges toward joining Hamlet in death through suicide. Earlier, Hamlet, as rationalist, must remind Horatio that,

> **Hamlet:** *Not a whit. We defy augury. . . .*
> (Act V, Sc. ii, line 215)

Yet, in immediate contradiction, Hamlet says

> **Hamlet:** *There is special providence in the fall of a sparrow. . . .*
> (Act V, Sc. ii, line 215–216)

and espouses mystical values and evokes mystical forces.

> **Hamlet:** *There are more things in heaven and earth, Horatio, Than are dreamt of in your philosophy.*
> (Act I, Sc. v, lines 174–175)

Throughout the play, this philosophic counterpoint oscillates as the two men alternate between medieval mystical wonderment and the emerging Renaissance humanism. In the end, Hamlet becomes the ultimate rationalist.

Through the Horatio–Hamlet dyad Shakespeare explores the challenges to medieval religious superstitions that marked the Elizabethan Age.[4] The Horatio–Hamlet dyad, like Shakespeare's England, struggles to free itself from the constraints and restrictions that medieval theology imposed on daily life and thinking. The fullness of this emerging freedom is loudly proclaimed at Ophelia's burial by

---

4 To the psychoanalyst, the dyad also explores the interplay between *primary process*, the mode of thought of the id with its qualities of timelessness and visual imagery, and *secondary process*, the mode of thought of the ego with its verbal representations, logical reasoning, and sense of time orderliness.

an unlikely character, Laertes. Without flinching, Laertes takes on the Catholic Church.

> **Priest:** *Her obsequies have been as far enlarg'd*
> *As we have warranty. Her death was doubtful;*
> *And but the great command o'ersways the order,*
> *She should in ground unsanctified been lodg'd*
> *Till the last trumpet: for charitable prayers*
> *Shards, flints, and pebbles should be thrown on her.*
> *Yet here she is allow'd her virgin crants,*
> *Her maiden strewments, and the bringing home*
> *Of bell and burial.*
> **Laertes:** *Must there no more be done?*
> **Priest:**   *No more be done.*
> *We should profane the service of the dead*
> *To sing sage requiem and such rest to her*
> *As to peace-parted souls.*
> **Laertes:**   *Lay her i'th' earth,*
> *And from her fair and unpolluted flesh*
> *May violets spring.[5] I tell thee, churlish priest,*
> *A minist'ring angel shall my sister be*
> *When thou liest howling.*
> (Act V, Sc. i, lines 219–234)

MASOCHISM AND ALTRUISM

The coupling of Horatio and Hamlet allows for exploration of a subtle aspect of identification. As psychoanalysis was formulating the role of defense in psychic functioning, Anna Freud provided an important codification of the defenses, which she called the ego defenses. In *The Ego and The Mechanisms of Defense* (1936) she discusses altruism and its relation to projection and identification. Her discussion is strongly weighted with considerations of masochism.

Little has been written about the role of masochism and altruism in interpersonal relationships. Whereas masochism is commonly linked to female psychology and female psychopathology, the original

---

[5] Violets, the symbol of faithfulness, are the flower Ophelia referred to as withering when her father died (Act IV, Sc. v, lines 180–183).

descriptions of masochism were of men coming under the spell of a woman and being forced into degrading self-depreciation in order to maintain the woman's love.[6] In describing altruism, Anna Freud had in mind a person, usually a woman, who surrenders herself to another. Using a child's governess as an example, Anna Freud saw altruistic surrender as the situation in which a person lives vicariously through the life of another with no authentic self-fulfillment.

Anna Freud's formulation of altruism does not clearly differentiate altruism from masochism and does not take into account the role of identification in altruism.[7] Her formulation does not acknowledge that as an individual identifies with the aims, goals, and achievements of another, the individual may be enhanced rather than diminished. In fact, self-enhancement is the essence of identification and altruism.

Anna Freud's altruism is a form of masochism.[8] Rather than identification with another, masochism is a manifestation of intense ambivalence toward the other (the sado-masochism dyad that characterizes masochistic relationships). Masochism may masquerade as altruism, but rather than a manifestation of identification with another, masochism is an intensely conflicted relationship with another with a variety of submissions, surrenders, and identification with the aggressor.

Viewing altruism as reflecting a high degree of self-cohesion and minimal ambivalence allows for identificatory self-enhancement and brings the psychoanalytic understanding of altruism closely in line with the Oxford English Dictionary definition of altruism. According to the OED, altruism is derived from French *autrui*, "of or to others."

---

[6] The study of a man under the spell of a woman was made famous in Leopold von Sacher-Masoch's *Venus in Furs* (1870), a strikingly autobiographic novel. Richard von Krafft-Ebing (1886) then used the male–female relationship in *Venus in Furs* to illustrate a form of sexual perversion that he named masochism, after Sacher-Masoch. With Krafft-Ebing's publications, masochism became a psychiatric diagnosis. Probably the best known derivative of Sacher-Masoch's novel was Heinrich Mann's *Professor Unrat or a Small Town Tyrant* (1905). Heinrich, the older brother of Thomas Mann, came to fame in 1930 when the film, *The Blue Angel*, based on his novel, starred Marlene Dietrich as the infamous Lola Lola and Emil Jannings as the pitiful Professor Immanuel Rath.

[7] Anna Freud tends to conflate altruistic surrender with altruism and does not distinguish between the two.

[8] Although is it unfair to "psychoanalyze" theoreticians from their work, anyone familiar with the life of Anna Freud might consider that she could be a bit harsh in her formulations of altruism. Without question she devoted her life to her father and the pursuit of his work and ideas. It seems likely that her emphasis on ambivalence and surrender in "altruism" may be autobiographically determined.

It was introduced into English by August Comte, the sociologist, to mean "devotion to the welfare of others, regard for others as a principle of action; opposed to egoism or selfishness."

HORATIO AND ALTRUISM

Horatio embodies altruism. His love for Hamlet is unquestioning, unconditional, and reciprocated. Throughout the play he supports Hamlet. Contrapuntally Hamlet and Horatio support each other in their attempt to remain rational in Elsinore Castle. Together they struggle to retain values and maintain reason in a corrupt world.

Horatio's support for Hamlet is put to the test as Hamlet tells him of Claudius's plot that Hamlet's *head should be struck off* (Act V, Sc. ii, line 25) in England. We hear how Hamlet, now a man of action, rewrote the commission naming Rosencrantz and Guildenstern as the recipients of that action.

Horatio ponders how this happened.

> **Horatio:** *How was this seal'd?*
> (Act V, Sc. ii, line 47)

Hamlet proudly proclaims, subscribing to a sense of foreordination,

> **Hamlet:** *Why, even in that was heaven ordinant.*
> *I had my father's signet in my purse,*
> (Act V, Sc. ii, lines 48–49)

Horatio's response,

> **Horatio:** *So Guildenstern and Rosencrantz go to't.*
> (Act V, Sc. ii, line 56)

can easily be played as though Horatio enjoys the thought of Rosencrantz and Guildenstern's getting their just deserts. However, Hamlet's response suggests that Horatio is aghast at what transpired and Hamlet feels he must defend himself.

> **Hamlet:** *Why, man, they did make love to this employment.*
> *They are not near my conscience, . . .*
> (Act V, Sc. ii, lines 57–58)

If the interchange is interpreted as Horatio's being aghast at what transpired, it suggests that Horatio is struggling with a greater tragedy than the death of their fellow students. He realizes Hamlet and he, like the rest of Elsinore's inhabitants, have been sucked into a mire of deceit and murder.

His response,

> **Horatio:** *Why, what a king is this!*
> (Act V, Sc. ii, line 62)

is his realization of the unrelenting misery and contagious evilness that the king has caused. He longs for the "good" king and the "good" age.[9]

Throughout the play, Horatio never questions and fully supports Hamlet. When Hamlet is wildly out of control, it is Horatio who calms him and gently returns him to reason. Hamlet's concerns are Horatio's concerns; Hamlet's sorrows are Horatio's sorrows. He identifies fully with his friend.

The fullness of the identification is dramatized in the last scenes of the play as Horatio watches his friend die. Horatio regresses from altruistic identification to masochistic desire to die with his friend. His thoughts flee to those of suicide.

> **Horatio:** *Here's yet some liquor left.*
> (Act V, Sc. ii, line 347)

Hamlet stops him.

> **Hamlet:** *If thou didst ever hold me in thy heart,*
> *Absent thee from felicity awhile,*
> *And in this harsh world draw thy breath in pain*
> (Act V, Sc. ii, lines 351–353)

Hamlet asks Horatio to continue for him.

> **Hamlet:** *To tell my story.*
> (Act V, Sc. ii, line 354)

---

9 A medieval quality is embedded in these thoughts. Implied is that the nature of a society equates with the nature of the king.

As Hamlet dies, Horatio's initial regressive response—to join Hamlet in death—quickly is transformed. He joins Hamlet in the realization of corporeal finiteness, and he knows that it is imperative that he be Hamlet's continuance.[10] Horatio is to keep Hamlet alive.

A second more powerful vehicle of Hamlet's continuance, Fortinbras, is about to make its heroic appearance. Fortinbras as continuance is made a reality by Hamlet's utterance:

> **Hamlet:** *But I do prophesy th'election lights*
> *On Fortinbras. He has my dying voice.*
> (Act V, Sc. ii, lines 360–361)

HAMLET AND FORTINBRAS

Fortinbras plays a shadowy counterpoint to Hamlet. As the play opens, we are told about the two princes. Mid-play Fortinbras appears in the distance, and in the ultimate scene of the play, he appears as the resolution. The two men never meet yet their crossing paths provide a basic structure to the play.

Tied together in political and mystical ways, Fortinbras in many ways functions as Hamlet's double.[11] Each is the son of a king and an heir apparent. Each bears the name of his dead father. Each is ruled by an uncle through unexplained succession. Further binding them is that on the day that Hamlet was born, King Hamlet killed King Fortinbras in battle.

As Hamlet leaves Denmark, a banished murderer, openly labeled insane, accompanied by betraying friends and on his way to certain death, he sees an advancing army.

> **Hamlet:** *Who commands them, sir?*
> **Captain:** *The nephew to old Norway, Fortinbras.*
> (Act IV, Sc. iv, lines 13–14)

Hamlet is told that it is Fortinbras on a mission.

> **Captain:** *We go to gain a little patch of ground*

---

10 Little does Hamlet know that his story will be told and retold perhaps more than any other created character in history.
11 Fortinbras's age is obscure. He could be older than Hamlet or younger by some months. The impression is that they are about the same age in a mystical twinship.

LAERTES, HORATIO, FORTINBRAS, AND HAMLET

That hath in it no profit but the name.
To pay five ducats—five—I would not farm it;
(Act IV, Sc. iv, lines 18–20)

The dedication of young Prince Fortinbras and his followers activates Hamlet's self-lambasting. He realizes that he is misusing reason—reasoning in order not to act.

Hamlet: *How all occasions do inform against me,*
And spur my dull revenge. What is a man
If his chief good and market of his time
Be but to sleep and feed? A beast, no more.
Sure he that made us with such large discourse,
Looking before and after, gave us not
That capability and godlike reason
To fust in us unus'd. Now, whether it be
Bestial oblivion, or some craven scruple
Of thinking too precisely on th'event—
A thought which, quarter'd, hath but one part wisdom
And ever three parts coward—I do not know
Why yet I live to say this thing's to do,
(Act IV, Sc. iv, lines 32–44)

In his impassioned self-search, Hamlet compares himself to Fortinbras.

Hamlet: *Witness this army of such mass and charge,*
Led by a delicate and tender prince,
Whose spirit, with divine ambition puff'd,
Makes mouths at the invisible event,
Exposing what is mortal and unsure
To all that fortune, death, and danger dare,
Even for an eggshell. Rightly to be great
Is not to stir without great argument,
But greatly to find quarrel in a straw
(Act IV, Sc. iv, lines 47–55)

His thoughts work into a masterful and remarkably modern anti-war proclamation.

> **Hamlet:** ... *I see*
> *The imminent death of twenty thousand men*
> *That, for a fantasy and trick of fame,*
> *Go to their graves like beds, fight for a plot*
> *Whereon the numbers cannot try the cause,*
> *Which is not tomb enough and continent*
> *To hide the slain? ...*
> (Act IV, Sc. iv, lines 59–65)

Fortinbras personifies identification with the lost father—he is a soldier like his father. His mission partially is to undo his father's defeat. Unlike Hamlet, who is mired in fragmented procrastination, Fortinbras is stalwart, courageous, decisive, and directed. He has assumed his father's role. He is his father's continuance—his father's immortality. Fortinbras represents what Hamlet might have been had he been able to identify with his father. As Fortinbras proclaims in the ultimate speech of the play,

> **Fortinbras:** *Bear Hamlet like a soldier to the stage,*
> *For he was likely, had he been put on,*
> *To have prov'd most royal;*
> (Act V, Sc. ii, lines 401–403)

INCORPORATION AND THE ARCANE

Rather than using the language of academic psychology, the psychoanalytic lexicon tends toward more metaphoric expression that reflects the visual language of the unconscious and the dream.[12] The psychoanalytic concept of *incorporation* and its more refined manifestations, *introjection* and *identification*, convey the subjective feeling of someone entering the personality as a continuing inner presence.

---

[12] Freud considered this mode of thought atavistic and termed it *primary process*.

The term *introject* describes the sense of an inner personal presence. Early in development the introjects tend to be global; the entirety of another is taken in. Such global introjects, abundantly seen in early childhood, are highly transformative of the personality and of varying endurance. During times of great anxiety or external threats, global introjection as a regressive phenomenon can become an epiphanic experience. Such regressive introjections are again of varying endurance.

The *identifications* are refined introjects that manifest as mannerisms, aspirations, and ideals of a psychologically significant other that have been integrated into the personality. Subjectively, the influence of the introjects feels alien, as though one is being driven; the influence of the identifications feels part of the personality and self-enhancing.[13]

During anxiety producing and compromising experiences, identifications may be regressively experienced as introjects. What was integral becomes felt as an alien inner presence. With further regression and failures in repression, the introjects may be re-experienced as all good or all bad, polarized negatives and positives, and may be projected onto the external as hallucinations and delusions. These psychotic hallucinatory and delusional experiences carry epochal and cultural intonation. Such severe regressions in certain cultures at times become atavistic experiences of being possessed and of visitation. The regressive experiencing of the identifications as internal presences or as spirits of another world is closely related to arcane religious concepts of continuance—the soul, the afterlife, and various kinds of reincarnation.

IDENTIFICATION AND MOURNING

Loss in the mature personality sets in motion a process of mourning. Mourning is characterized by an unbidden revisiting of shared

---

13 For the purposes of this discussion, I consider here only positive introjects and identifications. Negative introjects and identifications, that is, introjects and identifications associated with persons whom one hated, manifest themselves as hatred of the self or hated aspects of the self. Even more complicated are the introjects and identifications that are held ambivalently. The motivations for negative incorporations are multiple, complex, and often related to identification with the aggressor (A. Freud, 1936).

experiences and bittersweet reveries with eidetic memories (a regressive process) as aspects of and experiences with the lost individual are integrated as self-enhancing identifications. Viewed this way, identification evidences a high level of self-integration and differentiation and is a high order of defense against loss.

Mourning is a process of such vast importance for continuity of an individual and a culture that all cultures, primitive and sophisticated alike, recognize, esteem, and ritualize it. In fact, the rituals are surprisingly universal, regardless of the sophistication of the culture, reflecting the ontogenetic progression in personality development. These rituals often overtly represent ontogenetically (developmentally) early, oral incorporating wishes and experiences, the psychological basis for all such internalization. The most widely recognized of these symbolic cannibalistic rituals associated with loss are the feast of the wake and the Eucharist (Bergmann, 1992).

Viewed as a defense against death and the fear of finiteness, identification becomes the primary provider of personal and cultural continuity. Death not only gives life meaning, the fear of death is a major conscious and unconscious instigator of personal and cultural continuity. Loss and its alleviation through identification are essential for the transmission of human values. The fear of finiteness is a major motivator in perpetuating the transmissionable elements of being human. In the psychoanalytic idiom, these transmissionable elements are contained in the identifications.[14] In the Catholic idiom, they are contained in the Holy Spirit, symbolized beautifully as a dove entering from above. Although approached with different lexicons and from different historical perspectives, it is not surprising that in the evaluation of death and the warding off of the realization of finiteness, religion and psychoanalysis meet.

Yet, it must be recognized that even such a high order of unconscious response as identification is a denial of death—the denial of finiteness. Although the identifications provide continuance and are self-enhancing, they also involve limitations.

---

[14] The identifications comprise the ego and superego, the essential humanizing elements of the personality.

FORTINBRAS AND CONTINUANCE

Fortinbras personifies the virtues and limitations of unconflicted identificatory continuance.[15] Through identification, Fortinbras replaces, is enhanced by, and continues the father. Fortinbras embodies the new beginning and continues the past. It is self-enhancement; however, it also is limiting in that role, manner, and direction of the lost one become compelling inner presences of varying intensity at varying times.

As Hamlet watches Fortinbras, he at once envies Fortinbras's purposefulness while sensing fully the aimlessness and meaninglessness of Fortinbras's martial task. He knows that Fortinbras is driven by the inner signification of the land (a significance unconsciously and consciously tied to his father). Hamlet knows that Fortinbras's task is of limitless personal significance and at the same time is without significance, *a fantasy and trick of fame* (Act IV, Sc. iv, line 61).

Watching the advancement of Fortinbras's army has a profound effect on Hamlet. In Fortinbras Hamlet sees a dutiful son, a son fully engaged in an unconflicted identificatory idealization of his lost father. Hamlet's thoughts about Fortinbras put in broad profile how conflicted and stumbling is his path toward identification with his own father.[16]

> **Hamlet:** *Sith I have cause, and will, and strength,*
> *and means*
> *To do't. Examples gross as earth exhort me,*

---

15 Although we are informed that King Fortinbras was killed in honorable battle, Shakespeare presents no development of the relationship between Fortinbras and his father, his mother, or his uncle. Implied is that for Prince Fortinbras, in that the father has been heroically slain, whatever may be his concerns, King Fortinbras's death was without internal conflict.

16 Although generally ignored, at one point on his return from England as Hamlet is fully venting his anger toward Claudius, to our surprise, he includes anger about the succession. Even though Claudius promised Hamlet that Hamlet would succeed him, Hamlet reveals to Horatio that he feels on the death of his father he should have been king. For the first time Hamlet shows us something that Freud called to our attention, Hamlet's wish to replace the father!

> **Hamlet:** *He that hath kill'd my king and whor'd my mother,*
> *Popp'd in between th'election and my hopes,*
> *Thrown out his angle for my proper life*
> *And with such coz'nage—is't not perfect conscience*
> *To quit him with this arm? And is't not to be damn'd*
> *To let this canker of our nature come*
> *In further evil?*
> (Act V, Sc. ii, lines 64–70)

> *Witness this army of such mass and charge,*
> *Led by a delicate and tender prince,*
> *Whose spirit, with divine ambition puff'd,*
> *Makes mouths at the invisible event,*
> (Act IV, Sc. iv, lines 45–50)

In his self-search, he reworks his view of himself. He becomes "filled" with his father.

> **Hamlet:** ... *O, from this time forth*
> *My thoughts be bloody or be nothing worth.*
> (Act IV, Sc. iv, lines 65–66)

It is the reintegration of Hamlet, and he is transformed. It is a turning point in the play.

In the final scene of *Hamlet*, Fortinbras, as counterpoint to Hamlet, ends the play. Prior to his death, with the clear destruction of the old regime, Hamlet proclaims Fortinbras as the royal successor.

> **Hamlet:** ... *He has my dying voice.*
> (Act V, Sc. ii, line 361)

In the last scene, the Fortinbras–Hamlet dyad dramatizes the power of identification. Orderly succession and the transfer of power and values are assured. The king lives on in name and in spirit. The Hamlet–Hamlet is replaced by the Fortinbras–Fortinbras. The man whose son could not fully identify with his father is replaced by the son who is fully identified with his father.

> **Fortinbras:** *For me, with sorrow I embrace my fortune.*
> *I have some rights of memory in this kingdom,*
> *Which now to claim my vantage doth invite me.*
> (Act V, Sc. ii, lines 393–395)

In a psychological sense, death has been denied and at the same time defied. Finiteness is turned into infinity.

Madness and Hamlet

MADNESS AND MENTAL ILLNESS

The concept of mental illness arose during the late eighteenth century. As a by-product of the Enlightenment and the increasing scientification of medicine, madness became mental illness.[1]

To increase precision in understanding mental derangement, the new medical field of psychiatry divided mental illness into two large categories: neurosis and psychosis.[2] Although the capacity to function was an important consideration, major qualitative differences between the two categories were recognized. *Neuroses* are specific, often severe, mental impairment without major disturbances in reality testing; whereas *psychoses* are marked by major disturbances in perceptions of reality, particularly interpersonal reality.

Within the psychoses, a division was made between disturbances related to organic problems, toxic conditions and physical diseases affecting the brain, and disturbances considered functional in that the cause was obscure.[3] The functional psychoses were divided into disturbance in affect, that is, mood and emotion, and disturbance in thought. Disturbance in affect largely concerns mania, depression, and manic depressive disorders. Disturbance in thinking largely concerns schizophrenia.

---

1 The Enlightenment began the wresting of the care and treatment of mental derangement from the religious idea of sin and possession by evil spirits and from legal considerations of criminality. Mental disturbances came to be regarded as medical conditions with diagnoses, etiologies, prognoses, and rational treatments.
2 Psychiatry is the oldest of the medical specialties.
3 The obscurity regarding cause, etiology, led to many differing theoretical viewpoints regarding psychosis that continue to this day. These views range from genetic–physiological to psychological theories.

THE PSYCHOLOGY OF SCHIZOPHRENIA

Schizophrenia is a surprisingly common disorder about which a great deal has been written and about which there remains much controversy and disagreement. Psychologically, schizophrenia is a disturbance in development of the concepts of "self" and the "interpersonal other" (object).[4]

The self is a metaphor for the subjective sense of personal continuity, consistency, and direction. Sense of self arises from an enduring cohesion of internalized concepts regarding oneself and others. Over time the sense of self progressively requires less and less external validation. It is the integration of self-concepts with the concomitant integration and differentiation of concepts of others (objects) that allows for intimacy and self-transcendence.

Regressive tensions under various circumstances, often idiosyncratic to the individual, can undermine the sense of self-cohesion and self-differentiation. With regression, developmentally early concepts of self and other—highly rigid and polarized extremes of good and bad—are experienced with fear of self-fragmentation, self-annihilation, and nonexistence—existential anxiety.

In schizophrenia, literally splits (*schizo*) in the mind (*phrenia*), the self is largely fragmented and polarized. The resulting sense of self-fragility, fear of self-fragmentation, and the fear of fusion with other are often defended against by emotional distance, lability, outbursts, and by paranoid accusation.[5] Typically, feelings of emptiness, emotional vacuum, and impending doom with horrific existential anxiety abound.

Schizophrenia may be acute or chronic; that is, it may suddenly manifest itself or be insidiously progressive. Acute schizophrenic reaction at any age suggests that fragilities in the self were latently present.[6]

---

4 *Object* in psychoanalysis is a generic term that refers to the significant interpersonal others in one's psychic life. For most the critically important "interpersonal other" is the mother.
5 The "splits" in schizophrenia refer to inconsistencies in thought and emotions and are not to be confused with multiple personality, which is an hysterical state in which a person maintains multiple identities.
6 Precipitating events in schizophrenia must be viewed in a complex way. It is not simply a matter of quantity, that is, severity, but a matter of the idiosyncratic meaning of and the timing of the events interacting with latent tendency. This emphasis on latent tendency has a vague similarity to Goethe's "cracked pot" analogy, but it carries vastly different implications regarding dynamics and origins.

This brief summary of the psychology of schizophrenia is based on psychoanalytic developmental theory emphasizing the psychodynamic manifestations of schizophrenic processes. *Hamlet* is a dramatization of the intrapsychic dynamics of psychosis, not of its development.[7,8] As the play explores the psychodynamics of psychosis, *Hamlet* becomes a dramatization of the essence of being.

HAMLET'S MADNESS

As the play begins, Hamlet is angry, pensive, and bewildered. He has had to come to grips with a bitter truth—that his mother is deceitful, duplicitous, and untrustworthy.

The ghost of King Hamlet imparts terrible truths. Hamlet's initial responses are filled with eagerness and rapt desire to avenge his father's murder.

> **Hamlet:** *Haste me to know't, that I with wings as swift*
> *As meditation or the thoughts of love*
> *May sweep to my revenge.*
> **Ghost:** *I find thee apt.*
> *... Now, Hamlet, hear.*
> *'Tis given out that, sleeping in my orchard,*
> *A serpent stung me—so the whole ear of Denmark*
> *Is by a forged process of my death*
> *Rankly abus'd—but know, thou noble youth,*
> *The serpent that did sting thy father's life*
> *Now wears his crown.*
> (Act I, Sc. v, lines 29–31; 34–40)

Hamlet's response is of telling importance.

> **Hamlet:** *O my prophetic soul! My uncle!*
> (Act I, Sc. v, line 41)

---

7 There are, however, some allusions in the play that suggest a reconstruction of the genesis of Hamlet's disturbance (see Chapter 3, "Gertrude: Queen, Wife, and Mother").
8 This emphasis on psychosis and Hamlet is different from Freud's (1900) emphasis on the Oedipal love of Hamlet for his mother. Freud's interest in Hamlet's Oedipal conflicts led Freud to considerations along the neurotic spectrum—obsession, depression, and inhibition—rather than to considerations of disturbance in self. It must be remembered that in 1900 Freud was intensely interested in the importance of the Oedipal triangle in the development of the psyche and in neurosis. At that time, he had little experience with psychosis.

Shakespeare's use of *prophetic* suggests that intuitively Hamlet knows that his uncle, the man who married his mother and is now king, murdered his father.[9] The internal and the external become one. The ghost's voice becomes both a message carrier and the externalization of Hamlet's thoughts, the beginning of Hamlet's struggle in knowing what to believe—the beginning of the psychological ghost and the beginning of Hamlet's psychosis.

The ghost continues, ambiguously implicating the queen.

> **Ghost:** *Ay, that incestuous, that adulterate beast,*
> *With witchcraft of his wit, with traitorous gifts—*
> *O wicked wit, and gifts that have the power*
> *So to seduce!—won to his shameful lust*
> *The will of my most seeming-virtuous queen.*
> (Act I, Sc. v, lines 42–46)

Although it is not clear whether the seduction happened before or after King Hamlet's death, the charge *adulterate* suggests that the seduction was prior, leaving open the question of the queen's being an accomplice in the murder.

Hamlet's response is a forceful resolve to make the ghost's task his primary mission.

> **Hamlet:** ... *Remember thee?*
> *Yea, from the table of my memory*
> *I'll wipe away all trivial fond records,*
> *All saws of books, all forms, all pressures past*
> *That youth and observation copied there,*
> *And thy commandment all alone shall live*
> *Within the book and volume of my brain,*
> (Act I, Sc. v, lines 97–103)

His next thought is of great importance.

> **Hamlet:** *O most pernicious woman!*
> (Act I, Sc. v, line 105)

---

9 Freud (1900) took the term *prophetic* as evidence of Hamlet's unconscious wish to kill his father and marry his mother—that Claudius did what Hamlet wished to do. He further hypothesized that Hamlet could not kill Claudius because the king essentially did what Hamlet on an unconscious level wanted to do.

Hamlet's nearly unbearable anger with his mother quickly returns to Claudius. Yet, his anger toward Claudius seems almost an afterthought, one that can be written in his notebook (*my tables*).

> **Hamlet:** *O villain, villain, smiling damned villain!*
> *My tables. Meet it is I set it down*
> *That one may smile, and smile, and be a villain—*
> *At least I am sure it may be so in Denmark.*
> *So, uncle, there you are. . . .*
> (Act I, Sc. v, lines 106–110)

Hamlet's main concern is duplicity, subterfuge, and betrayals. In mother–child interaction, the deceiving mother is most damaging developmentally. Mother deception endangers the developing self. The Gertrude–Hamlet dyad rotates around primal disillusionment.

THE ANTIC DISPOSITION

When Horatio and Marcellus meet up with Hamlet, his response to them is erratic to the point that Horatio cautions,

> **Horatio:** *These are but wild and whirling words, my lord.*
> (Act I, Sc. v, line 139)

The fact that Hamlet's erratic behavior and talk precede his *antic disposition* is of critical importance.

The scene continues as Hamlet tells Horatio that the ghost is to be believed.

> **Hamlet:** *It is an honest ghost, that let me tell you.*
> (Act I, Sc. v, line 144)

It is interesting that even early in the play audiences so fully identify with this young man that they rarely doubt the veracity of the ghost's accusation, although no proof of Claudius's guilt is offered until his aside in Act III. As the viewer enters Hamlet's inner world, feeling what Hamlet feels, Hamlet's actions, including his inaction, become understandable. As William Hazlitt (1817) wrote, "his sayings . . . are as real as our own thoughts. Their reality is in the reader's mind. It is we who are Hamlet" (p. 164, 1963).

Hamlet reconstitutes and with full rationality says

Hamlet: *Give me one poor request.*
...
Never make known what you have seen tonight.
(Act I, Sc. v, line 148; 149)

But what follows is the frantic Swearing Scene. Four times the ghost calls out from beneath, three times the single word *swear*, then once *swear by his sword*. Although the stage instructions note that the ghost's voice comes from underneath, there is no indication that it is heard by anyone but Hamlet (and the audience). It can be effectively played that only Hamlet hears these calls. His erratic dancing around and irrational flippant calling back to the ghost are the introduction of the psychological ghost, Hamlet's hallucination.

Horatio attempts to calm his friend. He is somewhat successful until the ghost's first *swear*.

Hamlet: *Ah ha, boy, say'st thou so? Art thou there, truepenny?*
Come on, you hear this fellow in the cellarage.
Consent to swear.
(Act I, Sc. v, lines 158–160)

With the ghost's second *swear*, Hamlet's response

Hamlet: *Hic et ubique?* ...
(Act I, Sc. v, line 164)

suggests that for Hamlet the voice is coming from everywhere and nowhere—that Hamlet has lost all sense of what are his thoughts and what is external.

By the third *swear*, Hamlet is completely erratic and irrational.

Hamlet: *Well said, old mole. Canst work i'th' earth so fast?*
A worthy pioner! Once more remove, good friends.
(Act I, Sc. v, lines 170-171)

Although Horatio's response

> **Horatio:** *O day and night, but this is wondrous strange.*
> (Act I, Sc. v, line 172)

can be a response to seeing the ghost earlier and hearing his voice from below, it would seem more a responding to Hamlet's strange behavior and provocatively calling to an unseen and an unheard (hallucinated) ghost.

In the midst of this confusion, Horatio, the rationalist, is challenged by Hamlet.

> **Hamlet:** *And therefore as a stranger give it welcome.*
> *There are more things in heaven and earth, Horatio,*
> *Than are dreamt of in your philosophy.*
> (Act I, Sc. v, lines 173–175)

It is the first hint that Hamlet harbors mystical ideas, and it is the introduction of the curious interplay of rationality and mysticism personified in the Hamlet–Horatio dyad.

In response to Horatio's alarm during the swearing rituals, Hamlet develops his flimsy, fragile rationalization for the antic disposition.

> **Hamlet:** *Here, as before, never, so help you mercy,*
> *How strange or odd some'er I bear myself—*
> *As I perchance hereafter shall think meet*
> *To put an antic disposition on—*
> (Act I, Sc. v, lines 177–180)

He explains his behavior to reassure Horatio, and more so to reassure himself.[10]

The antic disposition serves Hamlet many purposes. Primarily, it is a kind of mastery, an attempt to gain control of something over which he has no control, his psychosis. By *put(ting) on* an antic disposition, Hamlet is changing passive to active; he is acting insane to control

---

10 Psychotics are frequently highly dependent on what they think others think, especially about their state of mind. As he explains to Horatio how he might act, Hamlet is reassuring himself about how he is. Frequently, and most clearly in Gertrude's bed chamber, Hamlet becomes terrified when he realizes that someone suspects that he has lost control of his mind. At those moments frantically he attempts to reassure the other person, thereby feebly reassuring himself.

his psychosis. The feeling of *put(ting) on* rather than its happening provides Hamlet with the illusion of control. The antic disposition is madness to hide and control psychosis.[11][12]

Although Prosser's (1971) arguments regarding Hamlet's antic behavior are limited regarding psychotic processes, her suggestion that Horatio's attempt to quiet Hamlet actually gives Hamlet the idea for the antic disposition is valuable. Prosser states, "Knowing himself, he (Hamlet) realized that he may act oddly and picks up the suggestion implicit in Horatio's puzzled responses to his erratic behavior" (p. 151). Adding a more complex psychodynamic interpretation to her suggestion, I suggest that Hamlet's antic disposition becomes an attempt to organize himself by seizing upon an idea given to him by someone important in his life at a critical moment. It is a vivid enactment of a transmuting, though fragile, introjection.

HAMLET'S *TRANSFORMATION*

Even though Hamlet's psychosis is clearly recognized by his mother, his uncle, the court advisor, Horatio, his school chums, Ophelia, Laertes, and himself, century after century scholars raise the question of Hamlet's sanity (Brandes, 1963; Levin, 1959). I suggest that as we identify with Hamlet, we rationalize away the obvious. As Hamlet's experience resonates with archaic, atavistic, anachronistic experiences that reside within all human beings, his irrationality becomes meaningful. As his psychosis is recognizable as an intrinsic part of being human, we enter his inner life.

Ophelia provides the first description of the changed Hamlet.

Ophelia: *O my lord, my lord, I have been so affrighted.*
Polonius: *With what i'th' name of God?*
Ophelia: *My lord, as I was sewing in my closet,*

---

[11] Although I propose that *Hamlet* presents and gives us insight into the psychodynamics of schizophrenia, generally I refer to the more generic term "psychosis" to obviate complicated technical discussions of variants of schizophrenia, such as borderline states, latent schizophrenia, micropsychosis, and borderline personality (Kernberg, 1975).

[12] Although the primary gain in the antic disposition is to control his psychosis, there are secondary gains, most of which are ineffective. It seems that in an exaggerated way Hamlet is hiding that he is a man on a lethal mission. The antic disposition allows Hamlet to vent vicious attacks on the king, the queen, and the court, erroneously thinking they will be excused or ignored because he is believed to be mad.

> *Lord Hamlet, with his doublet all unbrac'd,*
> *No hat upon his head, his stockings foul'd,*
> *Ungarter'd and down-gyved to his ankle,*
> *Pale as his shirt, his knees knocking each other,*
> *And with a look so piteous in purport*
> *As if he had been loosed out of hell*
> *To speak of horrors, he comes before me.*
> ...
> *He took me by the wrist and held me hard.*
> *Then goes he to the length of all his arm,*
> *And with his other hand thus o'er his brow*
> *He falls to such perusal of my face*
> *As a would draw it. Long stay'd he so.*
> *At last, a little shaking of mine arm,*
> *And thrice his head thus waving up and down,*
> *He rais'd a sigh so piteous and profound*
> *As it did seem to shatter all his bulk*
> *And end his being. That done, he lets me go,*
> *And with his head over his shoulder turn'd*
> *He seem'd to find his way without his eyes,*
> *For out o' doors he went without their helps,*
> *And to the last bended their light on me.*
> (Act II, Sc. i, lines 75–84; 87–100)

Ophelia is clearly describing a deranged man. Deranged, yes. But is he psychotic? Hamlet is acting the deranged man. In contrast with this early scene, in the Nunnery Scene, Hamlet's psychosis is blatantly revealed through his tormenting plays on words, condensed multiple meanings, blatant psychotic sadism, splitting, and barely controlled thoughts.[13] Similarly, in many scenes with Polonius, Hamlet's feigned madness is mixed with psychosis. Polonius ponders,

---

[13] "Splitting" is a difficult concept to understand. It refers to early and primitive defensive operations in which emotions (affects) are kept apart, split off, from an idea. Splitting often gives the psychotic a "flattened" quality, as s/he says horrible things without apparent emotion. At the same time, in the psychotic inappropriately intensified affect may be attached to various ideas giving an erratic quality to the thoughts. Often the idea and affect together are "split" off from the flow of thoughts. The thoughts appear jumbled, as unconnected "loose associations." Such looseness, although seemingly confused, at a certain level has associative connection.

> **Polonius:** ... *How pregnant sometimes his replies are—a happiness that often madness hits on, which reason and sanity could not so prosperously be delivered of.* ...
> (Act II, Sc. ii, lines 208–211)

Polonius puzzles about that which those who know psychosis know, that the thoughts of the psychotic, although seemingly erratic, are affect split off from thought and condensations of ideas and feelings on multiple levels—*pregnant*, as Polonius says. Their interchange ends with

> **Polonius** ...—*My lord, I will take my leave of you.*
> **Hamlet:** *You cannot, sir, take from me anything that I will not more willingly part withal—except my life, except my life, except my life.*
> (Act II, Sc. ii, lines 213–217)

Hamlet plays on the old man's words, twisting the literal and concrete. Polonius's word *take* becomes, typical of schizophrenic thinking, concretized and yet expressive of extreme feelings and dreadful thoughts.

Further and significant evidence of Hamlet's psychosis is the sudden change in his mood and behavior.[14] His greeting of Rosencrantz and Guildenstern is filled with hopefulness, warmth, and friendly jesting.

> **Hamlet:** *My excellent good friends. How dost thou, Guildenstern? Ah, Rosencrantz! Good lads, how do you both?*
> (Act II, Sc. ii, lines 224–226)

But when Hamlet innocently asks

> **Hamlet:** ... *But in the beaten*

---

[14] It is often difficult for those not familiar with psychotic processes to realize that psychotic reaction is contextual and hence highly varying. Psychosis is a dynamic state, not a static "illness." When psychotic propensity is present, the manifestations, though deviating widely regarding duration and severity, are largely a contextual interpersonal response. It is exactly that unpredictability in responding to people that earns the psychotic the appellation *mad* or in contemporary English *crazy*.

> way of friendship, what make you at Elsinore?
> (Act II, Sc. ii, lines 269–270)

Rosencrantz responds ingenuously. Hamlet questions further

> **Hamlet:** ... *Come, come,*
> *deal justly with me....*
> (Act II, Sc. ii, lines 275–276)

Guildenstern's answer is again tangential, and Hamlet angrily confronts the two men.

> **Hamlet:** *Anything but to th' purpose. You were sent for, and*
> *there is a kind of confession in your looks, which your*
> *modesties have not craft enough to colour. I know*
> *the good King and Queen have sent for you.*
> ...
> *... be even and direct with me*
> *whether you were sent for or no.*
> (Act II, Sc. ii, lines 278–281; 287–288)

Rosencrantz and Guildenstern pause, consult quietly, and confess.

> **Guildenstern:** *My lord, we were sent for.*
> (Act II, Sc. ii, line 292)

Clearly Hamlet is disillusioned by their deceitfulness—another betrayal.

> **Hamlet:** *I will tell you why; so shall my anticipation prevent*
> *your discovery, and your secrecy to the King and*
> *Queen moult no feather....*
> (Act II, Sc. ii, lines 293–295)

He begins a long and remarkably sensitive detailing of what he is feeling.

> **Hamlet:** ... *I have of late, but wherefore*
> *I know not, lost all my mirth, forgone all custom*
> *of exercises; and indeed it goes so heavily with my*
> *disposition that this goodly frame the earth seems to*

> *me a sterile promontory, this most excellent canopy*
> *the air, look you, this brave o'erhanging firmament,*
> *this majestical roof fretted with golden fire, why, it*
> *appeareth nothing to me but a foul and pestilent congregation*
> *of vapours....*
>
> (Act II, Sc. ii, 295–303)

Although it is easy to see depression in the hateful *foul and pestilent congregation of vapours*, actually Hamlet is describing a more profound sense, utter meaninglessness.[15] His helplessness with his state is perfectly captured in *but wherefore I know not*. With all that he could tell them, Hamlet can only express utter surrender to his state. It becomes an extraordinary description of psychotic decathexis of life.[16]

The next part of this discourse is of particular interest.

> **Hamlet:** *... What a piece of work is a man,*
> *how noble in reason, how infinite in faculties, in form*
> *and moving how express and admirable, in action*
> *how like an angel, in apprehension how like a god:*
> *the beauty of the world, the paragon of animals—*
> *and yet, to me, what is this quintessence of dust?*
> *Man delights not me—nor woman neither, though*
> *by your smiling you seem to say so.*
>
> (Act II, Sc. ii, lines 303–310)

This is the beginning of Hamlet's moving beyond the Renaissance glorification of man to a realization that the essence of man is existence—that man is but dust and that a man is only what he is and has been.[17]

---

15 There can easily be confusion about the relation of depression to schizophrenia. Depression can be a symptom or a diagnosis. As a diagnosis, depression can be neurotic or psychotic depending on the content. As a symptom, depression can be a part of any psychiatric disorder including schizophrenia.

16 Freud coined the term *cathexsis* to indicate the attachment of affect (emotion) to thought. It is the cathexsis that gives meaning to perceptions, ideas, memories, and experiences. Freud described how affect can be displaced or withdrawn as a defense against anxiety. When affect is withdrawn (*decathected*) from the perception of the external world including the interpersonal world, living becomes meaningless and people seem but puppets going through the motions of living. As a major narcissistic disorder, psychosis often is characterized by a massive withdrawal of cathexsis.

17 As noted earlier, *Hamlet* operates on medieval, Renaissance, and existential levels. This speech dramatizes the emergence from the medieval glorification of God to the Renaissance glorification of man. During the course of the play, Hamlet transcends to a higher realization—man is existence.

The confiding to Rosencrantz and Guildenstern takes an unexpected twist. The last statement suggests a paranoid process in Hamlet. He is now accusing Rosencrantz and Guildenstern of ridiculing him for homosexual tendencies. They are made uncomfortable by his accusation.

> **Rosencrantz:** *My lord, there was no such stuff in my thoughts.*
> **Hamlet:** *Why did ye laugh then, when I said man delights*
> *not me?*
> (Act II, Sc. ii, lines 311–313)

He clearly is confusing his thoughts with the thoughts of others. Although this major moment of bald paranoia in Hamlet is brief, it is another incidence in which self-doubt and self-criticism are externalized and become the thoughts of another.

Rosencrantz makes a quick and rather awkward retreat.

> **Rosencrantz:** *To think, my lord, if you delight not in man, what*
> *Lenten entertainment the players shall receive from*
> *you. We coted them on the way, and hither are they*
> *coming to offer you service.*
> (Act II, Sc. ii, lines 314–317)

Hamlet again is light-hearted, jocular, and inquisitive about the state of the theater.

> **Hamlet:** *Gentlemen, you are welcome to Elsinore. Your*
> *hands, come then. Th'appurtenance of welcome is*
> *fashion and ceremony. Let me comply with you in*
> *this garb—lest my extent to the players, which I tell*
> *you must show fairly outwards, should more appear*
> *like entertainment than yours. You are welcome.*
> (Act II, Sc. ii, lines 366–371)

But suddenly, he changes.

> **Hamlet:** *But my uncle-father and aunt-mother are deceived.*
> (Act II, Sc. ii, line 372)

Guildenstern responds

> **Guildenstern:** *In what, my dear lord?*
> (Act II, Sc. ii, line 373)

Both denying and revealing madness, Hamlet responds quixotically.

> **Hamlet:** *I am but mad north-north-west. When the wind is southerly, I know a hawk from a handsaw.*
> (Act II, Sc. ii, lines 374–375)

With the arrival of Polonius, Hamlet resumes his relentless baiting of the old man. It is never clear why he consistently makes fun of Polonius's mannerisms and humiliates him before others. Most likely Polonius is receiving Hamlet's loathing for Claudius and the devious older generation.[18]

Typical of Shakespeare, the interchange provides foreshadowings. Hamlet refers to Polonius as Jephthah, a man compelled to sacrifice a beloved daughter. (In Act III, Scene ii, Shakespeare tucked in that Polonius once played Julius Caesar, a foretelling of his being stabbed.)

With the arrival of the players, Hamlet is coherent, enthusiastic, and even jovial. While enjoying their recitations, although there has been no mention of doubt regarding the ghost since the Parapet Scene, Hamlet conceives of a way to verify the story of the ghost. His admonition to the players as they leave is revealing of his sudden shifts in thought and mood. One moment he castigates and humiliates Polonius, the next, he protects him.

> **Hamlet:** *Very well. (to all the Players) Follow that lord, and look you mock him not.*
> (Act II, Sc. ii, lines 538–539)

Alone with his thoughts, his *O, What a rogue and peasant slave am I!* soliloquy (Act II, Sc. ii, lines 543–560) is filled with inconsistencies and reversals. Although it is easy to see depression and anger turned toward the self, the disturbance is more profound.

---

[18] On another level, Polonius's hyperboles and redundancies are Shakespeare's caricature of the medieval style then rapidly becoming out of date. In *Hamlet* the generational conflict metaphorically represents the tension in the ending of an epoch. Polonius is the end of the Old (medieval period), and Hamlet is the beginning of the New (the Renaissance).

Hamlet: *Yet I,*
A dull and muddy-mettled rascal, peak
Like John-a-dreams, unpregnant of my cause,
And can say nothing—...
(Act II, Sc. ii, lines 561–564)

Unpregnant of my cause suggests curious decathexis, a schizophrenic splitting of emotion from ideation. His anguish turns to self-condemnation and self-derision as he fully realizes that only he is stopping himself.

Hamlet: *... Am I a coward?*
Who calls me villain, breaks my pate across,
Plucks off my beard and blows it in my face,
Tweaks me by the nose, gives me the lie i'th' throat
As deep as to the lungs—who does me this?
Ha!
'Swounds, I should take it: for it cannot be
But I am pigeon-liver'd and lack gall
(Act II, Sc. ii, lines 566–573)

The soliloquy ends with the formulation of the plan to verify the ghost's accusations using the performance of the traveling players. The expressed doubts regarding the ghost have merit, and yet they seem further rationalization for inaction.

Hamlet: *... If a do blench,*
I know my course. The spirit that I have seen
May be a devil, and the devil hath power
T'assume a pleasing shape, yea, and perhaps,
Out of my weakness and my melancholy,
As he is very potent with such spirits,
Abuses me to damn me. I'll have grounds
More relative than this. The play's the thing
herein I'll catch the conscience of the King.
(Act II, Sc. ii, lines 593–601)

At this point through an aside, Claudius lets us know of his guilt.

> **King:** *(aside)   O 'tis too true.*
> *How smart a lash that speech doth give my conscience.*
> *The harlot's cheek, beautied with plast'ring art,*
> *Is not more ugly to the thing that helps it*
> *Than is my deed to my most painted word.*
> *O heavy burden!*
> (Act III, Sc. i, lines 49–54)

The plot is set for Hamlet's deception by Ophelia. The stage clears, and Hamlet is alone. In the monumental *To be or not to be* soliloquy (Act III, Sc. i, lines 56–90), Hamlet is clear, rational, reasonable, and insightful as he explores co-existing states of being. The speech ends with poignantly tender thoughts as he sees Ophelia.

> **Hamlet** . . . *Soft you now,*
> *The fair Ophelia! Nymph, in thy orisons*
> *Be all my sins remember'd.*
> (Act III, Sc. i, lines 88–90)

THE NUNNERY SCENE

In the Nunnery Scene, Hamlet feverishly oscillates between irrational, barely suppressed hostility (displaced from his rage toward his mother) and affectionate protective feelings for Ophelia.

> **Hamlet** . . . *I did love you once.*
> **Ophelia:** *Indeed, my lord, you made me believe so.*
> **Hamlet:** *You should not have believed me; for virtue cannot so inoculate our old stock but we shall relish of it. I loved you not.*
> **Ophelia:** *I was the more deceived.*
> **Hamlet:** *Get thee to a nunnery. Why wouldst thou be a breeder of sinners?* . . .
> (Act III, Sc. i, lines 115–122)

As his hostility mounts, Hamlet becomes bitterly self-derisive and bitterly derisive of men in general.

Hamlet: ... *We are arrant knaves all, believe none of us.* ...
(Act III, Sc. i, lines 129–130)

Suddenly he asks

Hamlet: ... *Where's your father?*
(Act III, Sc. i, lines 130–131)

Ophelia lies.

Ophelia: *At home, my lord.*
(Act III, Sc. i, line 132)

Sensing deception, Hamlet becomes enraged and his mental disorganization is all too apparent to a frightened Ophelia.

Ophelia: *O help him, you sweet heavens.*
(Act III, Sc. i, line 135)

On fully realizing her deception, Hamlet scathingly denunciates Ophelia, a denunciation quickly generalized to all women. (As vitriolic as he is, it is but an attenuated preview of what will happen when he confronts the queen.) For Ophelia there is no question of Hamlet's madness. She is terrified by Hamlet's fully revealed, out-of-control mind.

Ophelia: *Heavenly powers, restore him.*
...
O, what a noble mind is here o'erthrown!
...
Now see that noble and most sovereign reason
Like sweet bells jangled out of tune and harsh,
That unmatch'd form and feature of blown youth
Blasted with ecstasy. O woe is me
T'have seen what I have seen, see what I see.
(Act III, Sc. i, line 143; 152; lines 159–163)

It is difficult to understand how those who maintain that Hamlet is not psychotic can read the Nunnery Scene and not be persuaded as to his mental state as his tormented mind oscillates between the irrational and the rational and rushes into vulgarly sexualized rages. In fact, a strong case can be made that the clearest description Shakespeare provides of Hamlet's feigned madness *versus* his psychosis is revealed by comparing his bizarre, theatrical behavior as described by Ophelia while sewing in her closet with his psychotic ranting in the Nunnery Scene.

The king secretly looking on is alarmed.

> **King:** *Love? His affections do not that way tend,*
> *Nor what he spake, though it lack'd form a little,*
> *Was not like madness....*
> (Act III, Sc. i, lines 164–166)

Although accurately sensing that Hamlet's thoughts *lack'd form,* he momentarily pushes aside the idea of madness. For Claudius, the pressing issue is that Hamlet is too dangerous to be allowed to live. Yet, there is no question that Claudius knows Hamlet is mad.

> **King:** *Madness in great ones must not unwatch'd go.*
> (Act III, Sc. i, line 190)

He then plots Hamlet's death.

Rebounding from the hurt of his encounter with Ophelia, Hamlet comes upon Horatio, the only one who has remained true and trustworthy. With Horatio, Hamlet again reconstitutes, and in touching discourse Hamlet thanks him.

> **Hamlet:** *... for thou hast been*
> *As one, in suff'ring all, that suffers nothing,*
> *A man that Fortune's buffets and rewards*
> *Hast ta'en with equal thanks; and blest art those*
> *Whose blood and judgment are so well commeddled*
> *That they are not a pipe for Fortune's finger*
> *To sound what stop she please. Give me that man*
> *That is not passion's slave, and I will wear him*

> *In my heart's core, ay, in my heart of heart,*
> *As I do thee....*
> (Act III, Sc. ii, lines 65-74)

Confiding in Horatio his plan to verify that the king is the murderer, for the first time Hamlet outwardly expresses doubt about the ghost and more importantly about his sanity.

> **Hamlet:** *... If his occulted guilt*
> *Do not itself unkennel in one speech,*
> *It is a damned ghost that we have seen,*
> *And my imaginations are as foul*
> *As Vulcan's stithy....*
> (Act III, Sc. ii, lines 80-84)

As the assembled court enters for the play within the play, Hamlet exaggerates his madness and plays the antic disposition full tilt. He baits everyone including the king. His banter is raw to the point that Ophelia says

> **Ophelia:** *You are naught, you are naught.*[19] *I'll mark the play.*
> (Act III, Sc. ii, line 143)

Hamlet becomes increasingly crass in his denunciation of Gertrude's infidelity. The antic disposition gives way to more overt psychotic expression.

> **Hamlet:** *... For look you how cheerfully my*
> *mother looks and my father died within's two hours.*
> **Ophelia:** *Nay, 'tis twice two months, my lord.*
> **Hamlet:** *So long? Nay then, let the devil wear black, for I'll*
> *have a suit of sables. O heavens, die two months ago*
> *and not forgotten yet! Then there's hope a great*
> *man's memory may outlive his life half a year. But*
> *by'r lady a must build churches then, or else shall*
> *a suffer not thinking on, with the hobby-horse, whose*
> *epitaph is 'For O, for O, the hobby-horse is forgot'.*
> (Act III, Sc. ii, lines 124-133)

---

19 *Naught* equates with lewd.

THE PLAY WITHIN THE PLAY

The Mousetrap play presents many possibilities for interpretation. Of importance psychoanalytically, Hamlet mislabels Lucianus, who murders the duke (Gonzago), as the nephew of a king rather than as the nephew of a duke.

> **Hamlet:** The Mousetrap—*marry, how tropically! This play is the image of a murder done in Vienna—Gonzago is the Duke's name, his wife Baptista—you shall see anon. 'Tis a knavish piece of work, but what o' that? Your Majesty, and we that have free souls, it touches us not. Let the galled jade wince, our withers are unwrung.*
> *[Enter Lucianus.]*
> *This is one Lucianus, nephew to the King.*
> ...
> *A poisons him i'th' garden for his estate. His name's Gonzago. The story is extant, and written in very choice Italian. You shall see anon how the murderer gets the love of Gonzago's wife.*
> (Act III, Sc. ii, lines 232–239; 255–258)

Mislabeling Gonzago as king brings the play closer to the ghost's report of what happened in Elsinore's garden. Further, it makes the nephew rather than the brother the murderer of the king. Hamlet is Claudius's nephew. The error becomes meaningful as a revelation of an identity in Hamlet's mind between Claudius and himself. In his parapraxis Hamlet reveals that unconsciously he is the murderer of the king. Condensed in the parapraxis also is Hamlet's wish that he, a nephew, could kill the king (his uncle, Claudius). Either way, the murderer (Hamlet) gets *the love of Gonzago's wife* (the wife of the duke/king).[20]

For Hamlet and Horatio, *The Mousetrap* effectively incriminates Claudius. With a mixture of excitement, confusion, non sequitur, rationality, irrationality, and dangerous bantering, bolstered by

---

[20] This is strong evidence for Freud's hypothesis regarding Hamlet's conflict and delay; however, Freud underinterprets, I feel, the identity of Hamlet and Claudius as being on a neurotic rather than on a psychotic level.

Horatio's validation, Hamlet asserts his confidence in the ghost's revelations and his own intuitions. Even though his confidence is fortified, Hamlet again is in a psychotic frenzied mixture of the rational and the irrational until he recomposes enough to say to Horatio,

> **Hamlet:** *O good Horatio, I'll take the ghost's word for a thousand pound. Didst perceive?*
> (Act III, Sc. ii, lines 280–281)

Hamlet and Horatio are interrupted by Rosencrantz and Guildenstern, who are sent to tell Hamlet that the king is very angry and that the queen summons him. Hamlet continues his bantering, interlaced with irrationality, until Guildenstern in exasperation says

> **Guildenstern:** *Good my lord, put your discourse into some frame, and start not so wildly from my affair.*
> (Act III, Sc. ii, lines 300–301)

Knowing that Rosencrantz and Guildenstern cannot be trusted, Hamlet with unadulterated frankness confronts them.

> **Hamlet:** *It is as easy as lying. . . .*
> (Act III, Sc. ii, line 348)

Using a recorder as metaphor he accuses the two of trying to *play* him in order to ingratiate themselves with the king.

> **Hamlet:** *. . . Call me what instrument you will, though you fret me, you cannot play upon me.*
> (Act III, Sc. ii, lines 361–363)

This electrified interchange is interrupted by Polonius, who bids Hamlet go to the queen's bed chamber.

HAMLET AND GERTRUDE

As Hamlet prepares for what is perhaps the most scathing denunciation of a mother by a son in literature, he fully exposes his hate-filled ambivalence for her, an ambivalence that is tearing him apart.

> **Hamlet:** *'Tis now the very witching time of night,*
> *When churchyards yawn and hell itself breathes out*
> *Contagion to this world. Now could I drink hot blood,*
> *And do such bitter business as the day*
> *Would quake to look on. Soft, now to my mother.*
> *O heart, lose not thy nature. Let not ever*
> *The soul of Nero enter this firm bosom*[21]*;*
> *Let me be cruel, not unnatural.*
> *I will speak daggers to her, but use none.*
> *My tongue and soul in this be hypocrites:*
> *How in my words somever she be shent,*
> *To give them seals never my soul consent.*
> (Act III, Sc. ii, lines 379–390)

Passing up an easy opportunity for revenge by killing Claudius at prayer, Hamlet proceeds to his mother's bed chamber. Strikingly free of psychotic ideation and fully concentrating on her infidelity and lack of shame, Hamlet accuses his mother of being an accomplice in the murder.

> **Hamlet:** *. . . Almost as bad, good mother,*
> *As kill a king and marry with his brother.*
> (Act III, Sc. iv, lines 28–29)

The murder is only lightly pursued in contrast to his intense preoccupation with her re-marriage. Clearly Hamlet is dealing with primal thoughts, his mother's sexuality and her deceptiveness.

> **Hamlet:** *. . . Peace, sit you down,*
> *And let me wring your heart; for so I shall*
> *If it be made of penetrable stuff,*
> *If damned custom have not braz'd it so,*
> *That it be proof and bulwark against sense.*
> (Act III, Sc. iv, lines 34–38)

In his scathing discourse he confronts his mother with her blindness to his father's virtue, integrity, and devotion.

---

[21] Nero hated and killed his mother.

Hamlet: *This was your husband. Look you now what follows.*
Here is your husband, like a mildew'd ear
Blasting his wholesome brother. Have you eyes?
...
... What devil was't
That thus hath cozen'd you at hoodman-blind?
Eyes without feeling, feeling without sight,
Ears without hands or eyes, smelling sans all,
(Act III, Sc. iv, lines 63–65; 76–79)

Visibly moved, the queen cries out.

Queen: *O Hamlet, speak no more.*
Thou turn'st my eyes into my very soul,
And there I see such black and grained spots
As will not leave their tinct.
(Act III, Sc. iv, lines 88–91)

As Gertrude capitulates to her son's accusations, rather than softening toward her, Hamlet's imagery becomes increasingly psychotically lewd, as though Hamlet were with Claudius and his mother in their bed.

Hamlet: *Nay, but to live*
In the rank sweat of an enseamed bed,
Stew'd in corruption, honeying and making love
Over the nasty sty!
(Act III, Sc. iv, lines 91–94)

Gertrude begs him not to continue. Hamlet can no longer stand the intensity of the sexualized hostility he feels toward his mother, and his rage turns to the king.

Hamlet: *A murderer and a villain,*
A slave that is not twentieth part the tithe
Of your precedent lord, a vice of kings,
A cutpurse of the empire and the rule,
(Act III, Sc. iv, lines 96–99)

An exhausted queen utters

Queen: *No more.*
(Act III, Sc. iv, line 102)

The ghost then appears. Showing Shakespeare's remarkable accuracy about his understanding of schizophrenia, Hamlet's anticipation of the ghost's scolding voice becomes the hallucinated voice.

Hamlet: *Do you not come your tardy son to chide,*
That, laps'd in time and passion, lets go by
Th'important acting of your dread command?
O say.
(Act III, Sc. iv, lines 107–110)

As the voice of Hamlet's conscience reaches hallucinatory vividness, Hamlet "hears" and "sees" the ghost.[22] Hamlet's conscience is projected externally.

Hamlet: *A king of shred and patches—*
...

Ghost: *Do not forget. This visitation*
Is but to whet thy almost blunted purpose.
(Act III, Sc. iv, line 103; lines 110–111)

The queen in anguish cries out.

Queen: *That you do bend your eye on vacancy,*
And with th'incorporal air do hold discourse?
(Act III, Sc. iv, lines 117–118)

Her simple sentence ends all arguments regarding Hamlet's sanity.

Queen: *Alas, he's mad.*
(Act III, Sc. iv, line 106)

So intense is Hamlet's ambivalence for his mother that he also projects protective, tender feelings onto the ghost.

---

[22] It is atypical in schizophrenia to have visual hallucinations, although during moments of acute agitation, the hallucinatory experience can become so vivid and so completely projected to the external that schizophrenics may "see" things, an embodiment of the projected thoughts.

> **Ghost:** *But look, amazement on thy mother sits.*
> *O step between her and her fighting soul.*
> *Conceit in weakest bodies strongest works.*
> (Act III, Sc. iv, lines 112–114)

Attempting to comfort her hallucinating son, the queen tries to reassure him.

> **Queen:** *. . . O gentle son,*
> *Upon the heat and flame of thy distemper*
> *Sprinkle cool patience. Whereon do you look?*
> **Hamlet:** *On him, on him. . . .*
>
> . . .
>
> **Queen:** *To whom do you speak this?*
> **Hamlet:** *Do you see nothing there?*
> **Queen:** *Nothing at all; yet all that is I see.*
> **Hamlet:** *Nor did you nothing hear?*
> **Queen:** *No, nothing but ourselves.*
>
> . . .
>
> **Queen:** *This is the very coinage of your brain.*
> *This bodiless creation ecstasy*
> *Is very cunning in.*
> (Act III, Sc. iv, lines 122–125; 131–135; 139–141)

Hamlet's anxiety rises as he realizes that the queen knows that he is psychotic.

> **Hamlet:** *My pulse as yours doth temperately keep time,*
> *And makes as healthful music. It is not madness*
> *That I have utter'd. Bring me to the test,*
> (Act III, Sc. iv, lines 142–144)

Fearful of his insanity, Hamlet attempts to reassure himself by reassuring Gertrude.

> **Hamlet:** *. . . Mother, for love of grace,*
> *Lay not that flattering unction to your soul,*
> *That not your trespass but my madness speaks.*
> (Act III, Sc. iv, lines 146–148)

He pleads,

> **Hamlet:** . . . *Confess yourself to heaven,*
> *Repent what's past, avoid what is to come;*
> *And do not spread the compost on the weeds*
> *To make them ranker.* . . .
> (Act III, Sc. iv, lines 151–154)

The queen responds,

> **Queen:** *O Hamlet, thou has cleft my heart in twain.*
> (Act III, Sc. iv, line 158)

It is not clear if Gertrude is anguishing over her actions or the realization that she has destroyed her son's mind.

Despite her being spent and fearful, as Hamlet leaves, he cannot control his hostility and continues the vicious sexual admonition.

> **Hamlet:** . . . *But go not to my uncle's bed.*
> *Assume a virtue if you have it not.*
> . . .
> . . . *Refrain tonight,*
> *And that shall lend to a kind of easiness*
> *To the next abstinence, the next more easy;*
> (Act III, Sc. iv, lines 161–162; 167–169)

His thoughts intensify and the images become vivid, near hallucinatory, detailed lewd sexual images. Again it is as though Hamlet is watching his mother and his uncle in their bed.

> **Hamlet:** *One word more, good lady.*
> . . .
> *Not this, by no means, that I bid you do:*
> *Let the bloat King tempt you again to bed,*
> *Pinch wanton on your cheek, call you his mouse,*
> *And let him, for a pair of reechy kisses,*
> *Or paddling in your neck with his damn'd fingers,*
> (Act III, Sc. iv, line 182; lines 183–187)

MADNESS AND HAMLET

In an attempt to rationalize (control) his psychosis, Hamlet proclaims,

> **Hamlet:** *Make you to ravel all this matter out*
> *That I essentially am not in madness,*
> *But mad in craft....*
> (Act III, Sc. iv, lines 188–190)

But his thoughts again jumble.

> **Hamlet:** ... *'Twere good you let him know,*
> *For who that's but a queen, fair, sober, wise,*
> *Would from a paddock, from a bat, a gib,*
> *Such dear concernings hide? Who would do so?*
> *No, in despite of sense and secrecy,*
> *Unpeg the basket on the house's top,*
> *Let the birds fly, and like the famous ape,*
> *To try conclusions, in the basket creep,*
> *And break your own neck down.*
> (Act III, Sc. iv, lines 190–198)

The queen pledges secrecy.

> **Queen:** *Be thou assur'd, if words be made of breath,*
> *And breath of life, I have no life to breathe*
> *What thou has said to me.*
> (Act III, Sc. iv, lines 199–201)

Somewhat reconstituted, Hamlet reminds the queen that he must leave for England with his two untrustworthy friends. His pity mixes with contempt as he removes Polonius's body.

> **Hamlet:** ... *This counsellor*
> *Is now most still, most secret, and most grave,*
> *Who in life was a foolish prating knave.*
> (Act III, Sc. iv, lines 215–217)

On Hamlet's exit, the king enters and demands to know what has happened. Despite her promise to Hamlet of secrecy she tells the king,

> **Queen:** *Mad as the sea and wind when both contend*
> *Which is the mightier. In his lawless fit,*
> *Behind the arras hearing something stir,*
> *Whips out his rapier, cries 'A rat, a rat',*
> *And in this brainish apprehension kills*
> *The unseen good old man.*
> (Act IV, Sc. i, lines 7–12)

again confirming that Hamlet is mad. On hearing of the death of Polonius, there is no question in the king's mind that Hamlet intends to kill him.

> **King:** *It had been so with us had we been there.*
> (Act IV, Sc. i, line 13)

Rosencrantz and Guildenstern are sent to find Hamlet. No longer having any respect for his old school friends, Hamlet with contemptuous baiting intermingled with psychotic non sequiturs, puns, and cryptic references exposes them as opportunists.

> **Hamlet:** *That I can keep your counsel and not mine own.*
> *Besides, to be demanded of a sponge—what*
> *replication should be made by the son of a king?*
> **Rosencrantz:** *Take you me for a sponge, my lord?*
> **Hamlet:** *Ay, sir, that soaks up the King's countenance, his*
> *rewards, his authorities. But such officers do the*
> *King best service in the end: he keeps them like an*
> *ape, in the corner of his jaw—first mouthed, to be*
> *last swallowed. When he needs what you have*
> *gleaned, it is but squeezing you and, sponge, you*
> *shall be dry again.*
> (Act IV, Sc. ii, lines 10–20)

Rosencrantz and Guildenstern bring Hamlet to the king, who barely can control his rage.

> **King:** *Now, Hamlet, where's Polonius?*
> (Act IV, Sc. iii, line 16)

At this point Hamlet seeming with nothing to lose and asking for banishment increases the king's fury. Flippantly he answers,

> **Hamlet:** *At supper.*
> **King:** *At supper? Where?*
> **Hamlet:** *Not where he eats, but where a is eaten....*
> (Act IV, Sc. iii, lines 17–19)

Hamlet, his psychosis barely controlled, continues baiting the king with cryptic comments and non sequiturs laden with multiple meanings.

> **Hamlet:** *... A certain*
> *convocation of politic worms are e'en at him.*
> *Your worm is your only emperor for diet: we fat all*
> *creatures else to fat us, and we fat ourselves for*
> *maggots. Your fat king and your lean beggar is but*
> *variable service—two dishes, but to one table.*
> *That's the end.*
> ...
> **Hamlet:** *A man may fish with the worm that hath eat of a*
> *king, and eat of the fish that hath fed of that worm.*
> ...
> *Nothing but to show you how a king may go a*
> *progress through the guts of a beggar.*
> (Act IV, Sc. iii, lines 19–25; 27–28; 30–31)

Ever more exasperated the king again asks,

> **King:** *Where is Polonius?*
> (Act IV, Sc. iii, line 32)

Hamlet becomes baldly vicious.

> **Hamlet:** *In heaven. Send thither to see. If your messenger*
> *find him not there, seek him i'th'other place*
> *yourself....*
> (Act IV, Sc. iii, lines 33–35)

Deeply embedded in this psychotic cryptic baiting is the dawn of Hamlet's acceptance of death, not as

> **Hamlet:** *The undiscover'd country, from whose bourn*
> *No traveller returns, ...*
> (Act III, Sc. i, lines 79–80)

but as

> **Hamlet:** *That's the end.*
> (Act IV, Sc. iii, line 25)

This realization of finiteness is to be re-worked in the Graveyard Scene in Act V and fully accepted as the play rushes to its climactic end.

Conceding, Hamlet tells the king where Polonius can be found. With feigned care and tenderness, Claudius announces that Hamlet must immediately embark for England. Hamlet responds with an utterance of profound relief.

> **Hamlet:** *Good.*
> (Act IV, Sc. iii, line 49)

Defeated, disturbed, and banished, Hamlet takes his leave, but not without a last jibe at the king. The jibe contains a thinly veiled acceptance of a painful truth, that Hamlet realizes that his mother is no better than the king. Addressing Claudius, Hamlet hints at an identification with Jesus. In a psychotic condensation of ideas he says,

> **Hamlet:** *... But come, for*
> *England. Farewell, dear mother.*
> **King:** *Thy loving father, Hamlet.*
> **Hamlet:** *My mother. Father and mother is man and wife,*
> *man and wife is one flesh*[23]*; so my mother. Come, for*
> *England.*
> (Act IV, Sc. iii, lines 51–56)

As Hamlet leaves for England, Claudius when alone tells that he has planned to have Hamlet killed.

> **King:** *By letters congruing to that effect,*
> *The present death of Hamlet. Do it, England;*
> *For like the hectic in my blood he rages,*

---

[23] Quoting Jesus, Matthew 19:4–6 and Mark 10:6–9 write: "Therefore a man cleaves his father and his mother and cleaves to his wife and they become one flesh."

And thou must cure me. Till I know 'tis done,
Howe'er my haps, my joys were ne'er begun.
(Act IV, Sc. iii, lines 67–71)

THE REINTEGRATION OF HAMLET

One of the most compelling trajectories in the play is Hamlet's course from despair into psychosis and his reintegration. A critical moment occurs in the queen's bed chamber when with anguished anger Hamlet confronts his mother. It is in the bed chamber that he is most blatantly psychotic. Also in her bed chamber he kills a helpless, innocent man. In this scene, his mother most fully recognizes the tragedy of her son's mental disintegration.

Following the murder of Polonius, Hamlet is hauled before the king and he baits the monarch. Embedded in his baiting is Hamlet's sealing his own fate. He responds to his banishment with one word, *Good* (Act IV, Sc. iii, line 49). At last released from his torment and burden, his psychosis ends. During the remainder of the play his thoughts are rational, composed, and organized.

As Hamlet leaves Denmark, there is a fateful meeting. He sees Fortinbras's advancing army. The psychological confrontation with Fortinbras and his self-search bring about a remarkable reintegration. Feeling fully Fortinbras's identification with his father and his father's cause strengthens Hamlet's resolve. When he uncovers the king's diabolical plot to kill him, an energized Hamlet turns the tables on his untrustworthy companions and takes advantage of his captors' friendship and desire to help him.

Escaping death, Hamlet returns to Denmark. He now views life and death in a new way. This new view is played out, given voice to, and refined in the Graveyard Scene. Fully accepting an existential view of life and death, unknowingly Hamlet proceeds to a preordained death.

6 Ophelia and Psychosis

The tragic Ophelia is one of Shakespeare's most poignant and pitiable characters.[1] Ensnared in a profound and unrelenting drama, torn between her father and Hamlet, unable to give voice to the affairs that have rocked Elsinore, confused and terrified by Hamlet's behavior and menacing ways, Ophelia by Hamlet's hand loses her father.[2] She finds herself caught in a whirlpool of deceit that reaches its zenith when she is used by her father and the king as human bait.

However tragic and pitiful, Ophelia is a full character with profound emotions. Her affection for Hamlet is clear, and there is strong evidence that it was reciprocated (Brandes, 1963).

> **Hamlet:** ... *Soft you now,*
> *The fair Ophelia! Nymph, in thy orisons*
> *Be all my sins remember'd.*
> ...
> **Hamlet:** ... *I did love you once.*
> **Ophelia:** *Indeed, my lord, you made me believe so.*
> **Hamlet:** *You should not have believed me, for virtue cannot so inoculate our old stock but we shall relish of it. I loved you not.*
> (Act III, Sc. i, lines 88–90; 115–117; 118–119)

---

[1] Although frequently accused of portraying females as weak, in fact Shakespeare fills his œuvre with women of strong character and virtue: Portia in *The Merchant of Venice*, Cordelia in *King Lear*, Lady Macbeth, and Portia in *Julius Caesar*, to name but a few.
[2] It is striking how frequently Shakespeare gives few clues regarding the mothers of some of his most developed young female characters, such as Ophelia, Cordelia, Portia, Miranda in *The Tempest*, and Jessica in *The Merchant of Venice*.

Deeply hurt by his accusations, Ophelia is terrified of Hamlet's insanity.

THE NUNNERY SCENE
As Hamlet approaches Ophelia in the Nunnery Scene, his tender concern is obvious. However, when they are together, Hamlet's anger mounts and his teasing and mild tormenting intermittently regress, revealing latent psychotic sexualized rage and disorganized thoughts.

> **Ophelia:** *My lord, I have remembrances of yours*
> *That I have longed long to redeliver.*
> *I pray you now receive them.*
> **Hamlet:** *No, not I.*
> *I never gave you aught.*
> **Ophelia:** *My honour'd lord, you know right well you did,*
> *And with them words of so sweet breath compos'd*
> *As made the things more rich. Their perfume lost,*
> *Take these again; for to the noble mind*
> *Rich gifts wax poor when givers prove unkind.*
> *There, my lord.*
> **Hamlet:** *Ha, ha! Are you honest?*
> **Ophelia:** *My lord?*
> **Hamlet:** *Are you fair?*
> **Ophelia:** *What means your lordship?*
> **Hamlet:** *That if you be honest and fair, your honesty should admit no discourse to your beauty.*
> ...
> **Hamlet:** *Ay, truly, for the power of beauty will sooner transform honesty from what it is to a bawd than the force of honesty can translate beauty into his likeness. This was sometime a paradox, but now the time gives it proof. I did love you once.*
> **Ophelia:** *Indeed, my lord, you made me believe so.*
> **Hamlet:** *You should not have believed me; for virtue cannot so inoculate our old stock but we shall relish of it. I loved you not.*

Ophelia: *I was the more deceived.*
(Act III, Sc. i, lines 93–108; 111–120)

Deeply moved by her poignant responses, Hamlet becomes viciously self-reproaching.

Hamlet: . . . *I am myself indifferent honest, but yet I could accuse me of such things that it were better my mother had not borne me. I am very proud, revengeful, ambitious, with more offences at my beck than I have thoughts to put them in, imagination to give them shape, or time to act them in. What should such fellows as I do crawling between earth and heaven? We are arrant knaves all, believe none of us. Go thy ways to a nunnery. . . .*
(Act III, Sc. i, lines 122–130)

Then suddenly he asks,

Hamlet: . . . *Where's your father?*
(Act III, Sc. i, lines 130–131)

Although it is open to interpretation as to whether Hamlet senses that the two are being observed, there can be no doubt that Ophelia's reply is a pitifully unsuccessful attempt to conceal her deception.

Ophelia: *At home, my lord.*
(Act III, Sc. i, line 132)

Her concealment becomes her confession. As Hamlet awakens to Ophelia's betrayal, he unleashes an anger of psychotic intensity.

Hamlet: *If thou dost marry, I'll give thee this plague for thy dowry: be though as chaste as ice, as pure as snow, thou shalt not escape calumny. Get thee to a nunnery, farewell. Or if thou wilt needs marry, marry a fool; for wise men know well enough what monsters you make of them. To a nunnery, go—and quickly too. Farewell.*
(Act III, Sc. i, lines 136–142)

Frightened by the intensity of his disturbance, in vain Ophelia pleads,

>**Ophelia:** *Heavenly powers, restore him.*
>(Act III, Sc. i, line 143)

The Nunnery Scene provides deep insight into Hamlet's psychodynamics. Ophelia's deception and betrayal are an attenuated version of primal deception and betrayal, the deception and betrayal by his mother. In his scathing denouncement of Ophelia, Hamlet's thoughts reveal his profound, repressed, and now emerging fear and hatred of women. Deeply embedded is his anger over his mother's shallowness and unreliability.[3] The scene anticipates the climactic confrontation with his mother.

>**Hamlet:** *. . . God*
>*hath given you one face and you make yourselves*
>*another. You jig and amble, and you lisp, you nickname*
>*God's creatures, and make your wantonness*
>*your ignorance. Go to, I'll no more on't it hath made*
>*me mad. I say we will have no mo marriage. Those*
>*that are married already—all but one—shall live;*
>*the rest shall keep as they are. To a nunnery, go.*
>(Act III, Sc. i, lines 144–151)

OPHELIA'S MADNESS

Despite the intensity of her interchanges with Hamlet, Ophelia's demise is not in response to Hamlet but to her father's death, intensified by the fact that Polonius died at Hamlet's hands. Adding to her agony is that the murder was in a fit of madness. For Ophelia, it is an incomprehensible tragedy. Through regressive and hallucinatory ways, she disavows her father's death and the events around her. Her thoughts become lewd and incestuous. She turns from every reminder of the events and seeks refuge in a tortured, highly sexualized fantasy union with her father, an hysterical retreat into a world of her making.

---

3   As Gertrude with sorrow and clarity early in the play says
>**Queen:** *I doubt it* (his madness) *is no other but the main,*
>*His father's death and our o'er-hasty marriage.*
>(Act II, Sc. ii, lines 56–57)

It is important to distinguish Ophelia's madness from Hamlet's self-fragmentation. Ophelia's madness is a kind of hysteria. *Hysteria* is a complex neurosis, a compromise formation that expresses the unacceptable wishes and the defenses against them, often through physical illness, such as paralysis or blindness. Hysterical symptoms reflect the sufferer's idea of the illness. Just as hysteria can ape physical illness, hysteria can ape psychosis. *Hysterical psychosis* reflects the individual's idea of "craziness." Hysterical psychosis typically is "crazier" in manifestations than psychosis. Ophelia becomes the typical mad woman—ranting, singing, talking nonsense, and rhyming non sequiturs.

> **A Gentleman** *(to the queen)*: *She speaks much of her father,*
> *says she hears*
> *There's tricks i'th' world, and hems, and beats her heart,*
> *Spurns enviously at straws, speaks things in doubt*
> *That carry but half sense....*
> (Act IV, Sc. v, lines 4–7)

In foolish song to the queen and Horatio, Ophelia speaks of Polonius's death. Her madness as hysterical psychosis expresses and denies unacceptable ideas and feelings.

> **Ophelia** *(sings)*: *He is dead and gone, lady,*
> *He is dead and gone,*
> *At his head a grass-green turf,*
> *At his heels a stone.*
> (Act IV, Sc. v, lines 29–32)

Hamlet's antic disposition also is an expression of an idea of madness, but underlying his antic disposition is impending self-fragmentation, a schizophrenic process. Hamlet acts "crazy" as a kind of pseudo-integration. Ophelia acts "crazy" to avoid thoughts and feelings.

When the king joins the ensemble, Ophelia's murmurs, although disguised, become vitriolic and aimed at him. It would seem that at some level she knows that the king is responsible for all their misery.

> **King:** *How do you, pretty lady?*
> **Ophelia:** *Well, good dild you. They say the owl was a baker's daughter. Lord, we know what we are, but know not what we may be. God be at your table.*
> (Act IV, Sc. v, lines 41–44)

At the king's mention of her father, Ophelia silences him and in song becomes anxiously lewd.

> **Ophelia** *(sings)*: *Then up he rose, and donn'd his clo'es,*
> *And dupp'd the chamber door,*
> *Let in the maid that out a maid*
> *Never departed more.*
> ...
> *Young men will do't, if they come to't—*
> *By Cock, they are to blame.*
> *Quoth she, 'Before you tumbled me,*
> *You promis'd me to wed.'*
> (Act IV, Sc. v, lines 52–55; 60–63)

Pointedly ignoring the king, Ophelia exits.

> **Ophelia:** ... *Good night, ladies, good night. Sweet ladies, good night, good night.*
> (Act IV, Sc. v, lines 72–73)

THE DEATH OF OPHELIA

Enraged by the news of Polonius's death, Laertes returns brimming over with thoughts of revenge for his father. When confronted with the horror of his sister's mental demise, he cries,

> **Laertes:** *O heavens, is't possible a young maid's wits*
> *Should be as mortal as an old man's life?*
> (Act IV, Sc. v, lines 159–160)

Ophelia addresses the individual participants in her private drama in silly songs and the disguised language of flowers. Her presenting flowers to various characters is filled with symbolic meaning and hidden language. Although the text is unclear as to who is being addressed with which flower (allowing for innumerable theatrical interpretations), the most overt repudiation is saved for herself.

> **Ophelia:** ... *There's rue for you. And here's some for me.* ...
> (Act IV, Sc. v, lines 178–179)

Rue is the flower of repentance. The question is, of what must she repent—her betrayal of Hamlet in the Nunnery Scene, her blind obedience to her father, her anticipation of suicide? Teasingly, Shakespeare does not let us know who the *you* is in the gift of rue or her next bequest, violets.

> **Ophelia:** ... *I would give you some violets, but they withered all when my father died.* ...
> (Act IV, Sc. v, lines 181–183)

Violets are the symbol of faithfulness. But with whom has she lost faith—King Claudius, Queen Gertrude?

The spring flowers serve another purpose. The play begins with Horatio and the guards on the parapet in the dead of winter. Ophelia is now presenting spring flowers. We are jarred to realize that four or five months must have passed since the ghost's charge to Hamlet. Suddenly we realize that Shakespeare has lulled us into losing track of time. Not tyrannized by a linear time frame, Shakespeare has made Hamlet's delay visible as the play enters Hamlet's inner state. Until this point, time has stood still; now with crescendo after crescendo the principals reassemble in various ensembles as time rushes ahead at a feverish pitch.

Ophelia departs with another nonsensical song that takes on full meaning in the context of what is about to ensue.

> **Ophelia** *(sings)*: *And will a not come again?*
> *And will a not come again?*
> *No, no, he is dead,*
> *Go to thy death-bed,*
> *He never will come again.*

His beard was as white as snow,
All flaxen was his poll.
He is gone, he is gone,
And we cast away moan.
God a mercy on his soul.
(Act IV, Sc. v, lines 187–196)

Through verse, she struggles to let go her father. What starts as *he will not come again* becomes *he is gone*. The song ends with the sad request that her soul be saved.

Ophelia: *And of all Christian souls. God buy you.*
(Act IV, Sc. v, line 197)

Her *doubtful* death becomes less doubtful. The doubtfulness is enhanced by the queen's lament to Laertes.

Queen: *Clamb'ring to hang, an envious sliver broke,*
When down her weedy trophies and herself
Fell in the weeping brook. Her clothes spread wide,
And mermaid-like awhile they bore her up,
Which time she chanted snatches of old lauds,
As one incapable of her own distress,
Or like a creature native and indued
Unto that element. But long it could not be
Till that her garments, heavy with their drink,
Pull'd the poor wretch from her melodious lay
To muddy death.
(Act IV, Sc. vii, lines 172–182)

Clearly, Ophelia did not attempt to save herself and allowed herself to die. In her death can be seen intention, irrationality, and chance condensed. Her death was unconsciously motivated, and in that sense her death was a suicide, that is, within the religious lexicon *doubtful*.

DEATH AND THE AFTERLIFE

Rather than mourning Polonius's death, Ophelia joins him. Like her brother, Ophelia's defense against the fear of finiteness is magical. Laertes attempts magically to undo his father's death through retaliatory action; Ophelia creates and enters into a magical fantasy. She is with her father forever in an illusion.

As a response to the fear of finiteness, most religions have codified and elaborated on the concept of a life after death—the afterlife. Few attempts to deal with fear of finiteness can approach the power of the idea of an afterlife, be it a life in heaven or a continuation through reincarnation.

The psychoanalytic concepts of introjection and identification provide a way of understanding the arcane concept of the everlasting soul. Introjection and identification, as defensive attempts to deal with loss, provide a kind of psychological continuance. The individual "lives" within the surviving person. Psychoanalytically, the concept of an afterlife is a regressive, defensive projection onto the external of the introject, an elaborate illusion of physical continuance (Freud, 1927). Although using vastly different lexicons and with differing implications and traditions, psychoanalysis and theology meet when dealing with the transmission of human qualities in the face of death.

7 Death and Hamlet

Hamlet is generally regarded as an Elizabethan revenge tragedy. Yet contextually, *Hamlet* is a composite, a condensation of multiple dramas.

Like a dream, the play makes visible an interweaving of substrates in various combinations. Like a dream, various characters become personifications of various qualities residing in various combinations in the substrates. Hamlet participates completely in all levels. He is the fullest character in the play, and he is one of the fullest characters ever created.

As the play progresses, Hamlet evolves into *typus Christi*. As the fated son with an incorporeal father, Hamlet, the same age as Jesus, is predestined to save the world from corruption. At a basic level, *Hamlet* is a Passion Play.

> **Hamlet:** *The time is out of joint. O cursed spite,*
> *That ever I was born to set it right.*
> (Act I, Sc. v, lines 196–197)

Like Jesus, Hamlet's doom is foretold (as Claudius and Laertes plot his death), and he is martyred for the salvation of humankind.[1] It is no surprise that the full exposure of Christian themes reaches rich clarity in the Graveyard Scene in Act V—Hamlet's confrontation with death.

---

1 Harold Fisch (1971) in an unusual study argues for an identity between Hamlet and Moses. Taking the Parapet Scene as the theophany of Moses on Mount Sinai, Fisch equates *the task* with *the covenant*. This is revealed in Hamlet's response to the ghost, *And thy commandment all alone shall live* (Act I, Sc. v, line 102). Unfortunately, Fisch does not carry his discussion further and argue for the typological identity of Moses and Jesus.

THE GRAVEYARD SCENE

Hamlet's return from England despite Claudius's plot to have him killed requires the king to devise another solution. His foil is the enraged Laertes, who is ready to avenge his father's murder by Hamlet. Together Claudius and Laertes plan the death of Hamlet, planning that is interrupted by the queen and her news of Ophelia's death.

Abruptly the action moves to the graveyard. The two gravediggers, master dialecticians, are arguing the role of volition in suicide. As is often the case in Shakespeare, it is the comic, the fool, and the insane who know the universal truths. One gravedigger makes snide observations. He notes that morality is determined by class and that theology bends to the privileged. Together they depict the moral turmoil and impending changes in the Catholic Church and society in Elizabethan England.

> **Gravedigger 1:** ... *If this had not been a gentlewoman, she should have been buried out o' Christian burial.*
> **Gravedigger 2:** ... *And the more pity that great folk should have countenance in this world to drown or hang themselves more than their even-Christen.* ...
> (Act V, Sc. i, lines 23–29)

In their verbal sparing one of the gravediggers drops an important clue. He refers to Adam.

> **Gravedigger:** ... *Come, my spade. There is no ancient gentlemen but gardeners, ditchers, and grave-makers—they hold up Adam's profession.*
> (Act V, Sc. i, lines 29–31)

The gravediggers continue with typical Elizabethan gallows humor when Hamlet and Horatio appear. As one gravedigger sings a ditty, he digs up a skull. Awakened are the eternal themes of death, rebirth, and the promise of the New Age as the play begins to show its Passion Play underpinning.

According to the "Legend of the Cross," when the hole was dug to support the Cross, the skull of Adam was unearthed revealing that mystically the crucifixion is taking place at the site where Adam was buried.[2] The Cross links to the Tree of Knowledge. Adam, the first mortal, is linked to Jesus, the first to defy mortality—resurrection.

I Corinthians 15:21–22: *For as in Adam all die, even so In Christ shall all be made alive.*

This mystery is represented in Renaissance art iconographically as a skull beneath the Cross.

Watching the gravediggers at work, Hamlet responds light-heartedly. In his jesting he mentions Cain, Adam's son.

Hamlet: *How the knave jowls it to th' ground, as if 'twere Cain's jawbone, that did the first murder....*
(Act V, Sc. i, lines 75–76)

The first murder was fratricide, Cain's murder of his brother, Abel. The motive was jealousy. The passage is a veiled reference to Claudius.

King: *O, my offence is rank, it smells to heaven; It hath the primal eldest curse upon't, A brother's murder. Pray can I not,*
(Act III, Sc. iii, lines 36–38)

Hamlet's light-hearted bantering continues, becoming mildly blasphemous.

Hamlet: ... *This might be the pate of a politician which this ass now o'er-offices, one that would circumvent God, might it not?*
(Act V, Sc. i, lines 76–79)

Another skull appears, and Hamlet continues his word play, making fun of politicians, courtiers, and lawyers. In a fruitless attempt to

---

[2] It is because of the unearthing of Adam's skull that the site of the crucifixion is called Golgotha, Aramaic for skull. The other name for the site commonly used is Calvary, a word derived from the Latin *calvaria*, which also means skull.

obtain a straight answer from the gravedigger, important biographical facts about Hamlet are revealed.

> **Hamlet:** ... —*How long has thou been a grave-maker?*
> **Gravedigger:** *Of all the days i'th' year I came to't that day that our last King Hamlet o'ercame Fortinbras.*
> **Hamlet:** *How long is that since?*
> **Gravedigger:** *Cannot you tell that? Every fool can tell that. It was the very day that young Hamlet was born—he that is mad and sent into England.*
> ...
> **Gravedigger:** *Why, here in Denmark. I have been sexton here, man and boy, thirty years.*
> (Act V, Sc. i, lines 138–144; 156–157)

It is astonishing to learn that Hamlet is thirty.[3] Until this point, Shakespeare has led us to believe that Hamlet is a young, vulnerable man struggling with a terrible fate. Before our eyes, Hamlet suddenly matures.

The discourse takes a solemn turn as Hamlet confronts death in a personal way. He is told that the skull he holds is that of Yorick, the king's jester, whom Hamlet much loved and who died some twenty-three years ago.[4] A profound change occurs in Hamlet's response to life and death. At that moment all that remains of Yorick is what *resides* in Hamlet. The interchange makes visible that only interpersonal relatedness provides perpetuity. Death and life as abstractions are realized as the play becomes existential.

While fondly remembering Yorick, Hamlet suddenly asks Horatio

> **Hamlet:** *Dost thou think Alexander looked o' this fashion i'th' earth?*
> (Act V, Sc. i, lines 191–192)

---

[3] It is of interest that in the first folio edition, Hamlet is 19 (*Hamlet Folio, 1.* Vol. II, 1623).
[4] Hamlet does not say how old he was when Yorick died. He talks about being carried on Yorick's back and kissing him. It sounds as though Yorick died when Hamlet was somewhere between ages six and ten. The story confirms the gravedigger's placing of Hamlet's age at around thirty. This is of symbolic importance because it is generally assumed that Jesus lived approximately thirty years. (Shakespeare, himself, was thirty-seven when he wrote *Hamlet*.)

Hamlet morosely continues.

Hamlet: *To what base uses we may return, Horatio! Why, may not imagination trace the noble dust of Alexander till a find it stopping a bung-hole?*

...

Hamlet: *... Alexander died, Alexander was buried, Alexander returneth to dust, the dust is earth, of earth we make loam, and why of that loam whereto he was converted might they not stop a beer-barrel?*
(Act V, Sc. i, lines 196–198; 201–205)

As though he becomes afraid of the profundity of his thought, Hamlet's affect suddenly changes. Using a silly ditty, he describes the eventual fate of the great Caesar.

Hamlet: *Imperious Caesar, dead and turn'd to clay, Might stop a hole to keep the wind away. O that that earth which kept the world in awe Should patch a wall t'expel the winter's flaw.*
(Act V, Sc. i, lines 206–209)

The depth of Hamlet's change is brought into broad profile by contrasting his deep awareness of the finiteness of life in the Graveyard Scene with his baldly Catholic ideas revealed in his first soliloquy in Act I. In the first soliloquy (recoiling from the realization of the shallowness of his mother but not yet burdened by the revelations of the ghost), Hamlet can only yearn for death. He is morose and contemplates suicide. He provides a clear picture of his view of an anthropomorphic *Everlasting*.

Hamlet: *O that this too too sullied flesh would melt, Thaw and resolve itself into a dew, Or that the Everlasting had not fix'd His canon 'gainst self-slaughter. O God! God! How weary, stale, flat, and unprofitable Seem to me all the uses of this world!*
(Act I, Sc. ii, lines 129–134)

The soliloquy portrays a pensive young man with a conventional theological view of the afterlife and the punishments that come from not living within God's rules. His views are highly syntonic to the religion of his time.

In the graveyard, Hamlet expresses his full realization of the finiteness of death, that what one might have been or thought one was is of little consequence to eternity. It is this realization of the finiteness of death that Hamlet approached earlier but backed away from when he asked the central existential question

> **Hamlet:** *To be, or not to be, . . .*
> (Act III, Sc. i, line 56)

This singularly famous line uniquely and economically polarizes life and death. In six monosyllabic words Hamlet, rising above physicality, fully epitomizes the psychological essence of the basic biological polarity—life and death. There can be existential death in life and existential continuance in death. The crucial polarity of life is being and not being, a realization Hamlet struggles in the soliloquy to sustain but cannot hold. As his thoughts progress, *not to be* becomes *to die* and quietly slips into the attenuated version *to sleep*.

At this point in the soliloquy there is a break in Hamlet's thoughts that is marked by the simple utterance, *No more*. This is a *no more* with multiple meanings. On one level, the *No more* expresses the essence of nonexistence. At the same time, Hamlet's mind recoils from the realization of nonexistence, and he attempts to stop the spasms of thought. Hamlet longs for a death without mentation but fears a tormented death, an afterlife.

> **Hamlet:** *But that the dread of something after death,*
> *The undiscover'd country, from whose bourn*
> *No traveler returns, puzzles the will,*
> *And makes us rather bear those ills we have*
> *Than fly to others that we know not of?*
> (Act III, Sc. i, lines 78–82)

In the graveyard Hamlet leaves medieval Catholicism forever. Paradoxically just as he is about to embark on a reenactment of the most influential progression in the Western world, the Passion of Jesus with its climactic Resurrection, Hamlet comes to the full realization of the finiteness of life. Hamlet, who has experienced the reality of nothingness (self-annihilation in psychosis) transcends death by fully understanding death. Through vastly different metaphors, Hamlet and Jesus transcend death. Jesus lives on in the hearts of those who follow him, the Pentecost (identification in the purest sense). Hamlet lives on in Western thought because he touches universal truth.

OPHELIA'S FUNERAL

In the graveyard the interplay regarding Christian morality reappears between the priest and Laertes on a theologically rigid level. The argument is between form and substance, between righteousness and observance.

> **Priest:** *She should in ground unsanctified been lodg'd*
> *Till the last trumpet: for charitable prayers*
> *Shards, flints, and pebbles should be thrown on her.*
> ...
> **Laertes:** *... I tell thee, churlish priest,*
> *A minist'ring angel shall my sister be*
> *When thou liest howling.*
> (Act V, Sc. i, lines 222–224; 233–235)

In a dramatic moment, the discourse is changed when Hamlet identifies himself, and he and Laertes grapple in Ophelia's grave. Hamlet is surprisingly physically threatening.

> **Hamlet:** *I prithee take thy fingers from my throat,*
> *For though I am not splenative and rash,*
> *Yet have I in me something dangerous,*
> *Which let thy wisdom fear. Hold off thy hand.*
> (Act V, Sc. i, lines 253–256)

Taking Hamlet's side, the queen attempts to intervene as her son becomes grandiloquent in his proclamation of his love for Ophelia.

Gertrude tries to quiet Laertes by ascribing Hamlet's actions to *mere madness* (Act V., Sc. i, line 279), while Claudius quietly reminds Laertes that he will soon have his revenge. All exit save Horatio and Hamlet.

Recalling the monumental events that have befallen him, Hamlet admits to doubts and inner conflict.

> **Hamlet:** *Sir, in my heart there was a kind of fighting*
> *That would not let me sleep....*
> (Act V, Sc. ii, lines 4–5)

The sense of foreordination becomes clear.

> **Hamlet:** *... and that should learn us*
> *There's a divinity that shapes our ends,*
> *Rough-hew them how we will—*
> (Act V, Sc. ii, lines 9–11)

OSRIC, THE MESSENGER OF DEATH

The sense of foreordination heightens with the arrival of Osric, the king's messenger for whom Hamlet has nothing but contempt. After much flowery talk and praise of Laertes, Osric tells Hamlet that the king has laid a wager on him and he is to duel Laertes with rapier and dagger, weapons with which Laertes is an acknowledged expert. Resignedly, Hamlet agrees to the match.

> **Hamlet:** *... I will win for him and I*
> *can; if not, I will gain nothing but my shame and*
> *the odd hits.*
> (Act V, Sc. ii, lines 173–175)

Horatio knows something is wrong and cautions,

> **Horatio:** *You will lose, my lord.*
> (Act V, Sc. ii, line 205)

Hamlet, pretending that he has no fear, says,

> **Hamlet:** *... Since he went into France, I have*
> *been in continual practice....*
> (Act V, Sc. ii, lines 206–207)

but Hamlet has clear doubts.

> **Hamlet:** *Thou wouldst not think how ill all's here about my heart; but it is no matter.*
> ...
> *It is but foolery, but it is such a kind of gaingiving as would perhaps trouble a woman.*
> (Act V, Sc. ii, lines 208–209; 211–212)

Horatio tries to dissuade him.

> **Horatio:** *If your mind dislike anything, obey it. I will forestall their repair hither and say you are not fit.*
> (Act V, Sc. ii, lines 213–214)

At once refuting a belief in signs foretelling the future, Hamlet replies,

> **Hamlet:** *Not a whit. We defy augury. . . .*
> (Act V, Sc. ii, line 215)

and calling upon St. Matthew (X, 29) for his metaphor, Hamlet gives himself completely to predestination and the sense of cosmic purposefulness.

> **Hamlet:** *. . . There is special providence in the fall of a sparrow. . . .*
> (Act V, Sc. ii, lines 215–216)

Proclaiming the utter nothingness in death, he again asserts that being and death are polarities, and he readies himself for what may come.

> **Hamlet:** *. . . If it be now, 'tis not to come; if it be not to come, it will be now; if it be not now, yet it will come. The readiness is all. Since no man, of aught he leaves, knows aught, what is't to leave betimes? Let be.*
> (Act V, Sc. ii, lines 216–220)

THE DUEL SCENE AND CHRISTIAN THEMES

The Duel Scene poses many problems dramatically and psychologically (Eliot, 1920; Jones 1949). Why does Hamlet enter into a duel arranged by a man who he knows has plotted to have him killed and with a man whose father he has killed and whose sister he has driven to a horrible fate?

It seems that Hamlet foolishly is entering into something that can only lead to his destruction. His boast,

> **Hamlet:** . . . *I have been in continual practice. I shall win at the odds.*
> (Act V, Sc. ii, lines 206–207)

suggests a naïve dismissal.

When the king brings Laertes to Hamlet, Hamlet asks for forgiveness and attempts to explain that what he did was in madness.[5]

> **Hamlet:** *Give me your pardon, sir. I have done you wrong;*
> *But pardon't as you are a gentleman.*
> *This presence knows, and you must needs have heard,*
> *How I am punish'd with a sore distraction.*
> *What I have done*
> *That might your nature, honour, and exception*
> *Roughly awake, I here proclaim was madness.*
> *Was't Hamlet wrong'd Laertes? Never Hamlet.*
> *If Hamlet from himself be ta'en away,*
> *And when he's not himself does wrong Laertes,*
> *Then Hamlet does it not, Hamlet denies it.*
> *Who does it then? His madness. If't be so,*
> *Hamlet is of the faction that is wrong'd;*
> *His madness is poor Hamlet's enemy.*
> *Sir, in this audience,*
> *Let my disclaiming from a purpos'd evil*
> *Free me so far in your most generous thoughts*

---

[5] In view of this self-proclamation, it is astonishing that doubt continues in the literature about the authenticity of Hamlet's psychosis (madness).

> *That I have shot my arrow o'er the house*
> *And hurt my brother.*
> (Act V, Sc. ii, lines 222–240)

Knowing that his revenge will come, Laertes pretends to be satisfied.

> **Laertes:** *... But till that time*
> *I do receive your offer'd love like love*
> *And will not wrong it.*
> (Act V, Sc. ii, lines 246–248)

Hamlet continues, intimating that he knows that he will be defeated in the match.

> **Hamlet:** *I'll be your foil, Laertes. In mine ignorance*
> *Your skill shall like a star i'th' darkest night*
> *Stick fiery off indeed.*
> (Act V, Sc. ii, lines 252–254)

To the king he says,

> **Hamlet:** *Your Grace has laid the odds o'th' weaker side.*
> (Act V, Sc. ii, line 258)

The formality of the duel proceeds.

Weighing in Christian symbology, the Duel Scene becomes understandable to the play's rapidly approaching climax. I suggest that the duel with its inevitable end in the death of Hamlet is a veiled version of Jesus's (and Mary's) prophetic vision that He is predestined to be martyred.[6] On this level Osric is the visitation of the Angel of Death, the foreteller of the murder of the first-born son (Bergmann, 1992). Osric facilitates the fulfillment of Hamlet's preordained martyrdom.

> **Osric:** *... My lord, his Majesty bade me*
> *signify to you that a has laid a great wager on your*
> *head....*
> (Act V, Sc. ii, lines 100–102)

---

[6] Gertrude's acquiescence to the duel becomes a vicarious (an unconscious) condonement of Hamlet's inevitable destruction.

The Angel of Death, Osric, is to become the duel's referee.

Thinly veiled in the progression of the duel are symbols that read from the New Testament. Hamlet's return to the court is the entry of Jesus into Jerusalem. During the duel are clear references from the Fourteen Stations of the Cross. Identifying Hamlet as *typus Christi*, Hamlet meets his mother (Jesus meets His mother), the Fourth Station; Gertrude wipes Hamlet's face with a cloth (Veronica wipes the face of Jesus), the Sixth Station. The wounding of Hamlet by Laertes keys to the centurion's stabbing the side of Jesus. Of ultimate importance, on the death of Hamlet the arrival of Fortinbras as the heir to the New Age keys to the Resurrection.

> **Fortinbras:** *For me, with sorrow I embrace my fortune.*
> (Act V, Sc. ii, line 393)

Laertes' wounding of Hamlet carries implications beyond Jesus linking Hamlet to Adam. Seen as the spear wound of Jesus by the centurion, the wound in Hamlet's (Jesus's) side becomes the mark of Adam—the site of the emergence of Eve. Adam (the primal mortal), Jesus, and Hamlet become one. Building on the Graveyard Scene and the uncovering of the skull, Hamlet typologically joins Adam, the primal mortal, and Jesus, the personification of resurrection. Adam "lives" through his issue, all subsequent mankind; Jesus "lives" in the hearts of his followers, Resurrection; and Hamlet "lives" in the birth of the New Age, Fortinbras. Each symbolizes death. Each continues through death. Each personifies death, rebirth, and immortality. Death gives meaning to life, and fear of death activates continuance.

THE DEATH OF HAMLET

Returning to the play's narration, as the duel commences, Laertes in an aside expresses misgivings.

> **Laertes:** *And yet it is almost against my conscience.*
> (Act V, Sc. ii, line 300)

His misgivings may have impaired his ability, which may account for Hamlet's victory in the first set. As though asking for death, in the second set Hamlet encourages Laertes.

DEATH AND HAMLET

> **Hamlet:** *I pray you pass with your best violence.*
> (Act V, Sc. ii, line 302)

Hamlet is then mortally wounded. In a scuffle, the rapiers are exchanged, and Hamlet wounds Laertes with the poisoned sword. Realizing that he is fatally poisoned, Laertes confides to Osric his regret.

> **Laertes:** *Why, as a woodcock to mine own springe, Osric.*
> *I am justly kill'd with mine own treachery.*
> (Act V, Sc. ii, lines 312–313)

In the background, the queen falls and Claudius tries to distract attention from her.

> **King:** *She swoons to see them bleed.*
> (Act V, Sc. ii, line 314)

The balance suddenly shifts when the queen cries out,

> **Queen:** *. . . the drink! O my dear Hamlet!*
> *I am poison'd.*
> (Act V, Sc. ii, lines 315–316)

and the dying Laertes laments,

> **Laertes:** *It is here, Hamlet. Hamlet, thou art slain.*
> *No medicine in the world can do thee good;*
> *In thee there is not half an hour's life.*
> *The treacherous instrument is in thy hand,*
> *Unbated and envenom'd. The foul practice*
> *Hath turn'd itself on me. Lo, here I lie,*
> *Never to rise again. Thy mother's poison'd.*
> *I can no more. The King—the King's to blame.*
> (Act V, Sc. ii, lines 319–326)

Realizing that he is mortally wounded, Hamlet stabs Claudius with the poisoned sword and forcefully pours the remaining poisoned wine down his uncle's throat. Thus, King Hamlet's commandment is completed; however, the revenge cycle remains incomplete. Claudius's guilt is not revealed. Hamlet's last words to Claudius are curiously ironic.

Hamlet: *Follow my mother.*
(Act V, Sc. ii, line 332)

Does he believe that he is sending Claudius to be with her, confirming his suspicions that she was an accomplice[7]?

Laertes cries out, asking Hamlet for forgiveness. In an exchange of forgivenesses, Hamlet responds,

Hamlet: *Heaven make thee free of it....*
(Act V, Sc. ii, line 337)

and touchingly says,

Hamlet: *... I follow thee.*
(Act V, Sc. ii, line 337)

The farewell to his mother is indeed brief and marked by ambivalence.

Hamlet: *... Wretched queen, adieu.*
(Act V, Sc. ii, line 338)

Recognizing the immutability of death, Hamlet says,

Hamlet: *... —as this fell sergeant, Death,*
Is strict in his arrest—...
(Act V, Sc. ii, lines 341–342)

and asks Horatio to

Hamlet: *... Report me and my cause aright*
(Act V, Sc. ii, line 344)

Having lost confidence in the rationality that he early on professed, Horatio cries out,

---

7 This is a nonpsychotic version of the curious interplay between the king and Hamlet in Act IV:

> **Hamlet** (to the king): *Farewell, dear mother.*
> **King:** *Thy loving father, Hamlet.*
> **Hamlet:** *My mother. Father and mother is man and wife,*
> *man and wife is one flesh; so my mother. Come, for*
> *England.*
> (Act IV, Sc. iii, lines 52–56)

Hamlet is implying that Claudius and Gertrude are of the same ilk and that they deserve each other.

> **Horatio:** *I am more an antique Roman than a Dane.*
> (Act V, Sc. ii, line 346)

and moves to drink from the poisoned cup. Hamlet implores him.

> **Hamlet:** *If thou didst ever hold me in thy heart,*
> *Absent thee from felicity awhile,*
> *And in this harsh world draw thy breath in pain*
> *To tell my story.*
> (Act V, Sc. ii, lines 351–354)

It is Osric, the Angel of Death, who now becomes the bearer of the Glad Tidings. He announces the arrival of the conquering Fortinbras; whereupon, Hamlet proclaims his desire that Fortinbras be the new king.

> **Hamlet:** *I do prophesy th'election lights*
> *On Fortinbras. He has my dying voice.*
> (Act V, Sc. ii, lines 360–361)

THE LAST WORDS OF HAMLET

> **Hamlet:** . . . —*the rest is silence.*
> (Act V, Sc. ii, line 363)

brings to closure the struggle that ensues within Hamlet throughout the play—the struggle between the deistic theology of the medieval period and an existential acceptance of life. In *The rest is silence,* there is no illusion of or plea for continuance; there is the full acceptance that there is *no more.* Horatio, the consummate rationalist, and Hamlet, the questioner of such certainty, within the progression of the play frequently alternate their positions. Yet by the play's conclusion, the two assume the opposite polarity. Hamlet is the existentialist and Horatio the preordinationist.

HAMLET AND JESUS: THE ULTIMATE PARADOX

How can we reconcile *Hamlet's* Passion Play subscript with the clear rush toward a preordination with Hamlet's final heartcry? In fact, the same paradox exists in the Passion itself. On the Cross, Jesus's sense of preordination carries him until the ninth hour. As death approaches, Jesus calls out, *Eloi, Eloi, lama sabachthani?* This agonal cry is generally interpreted as *My God, My God, why has Thou forsaken me?* (Mark, 34; Matthew, 46) and deservedly is heavily interpreted and debated.

The Gospels of Mark and Matthew both agree about the timing of the utterance and the Hebrew quotation. Luke presents a markedly different version. Luke reports Jesus's final outcry as, *Father into Thy hands I commend My spirit* (Luke, 46) (The Washburn College Bible, 1980). The Gospel of John does not record the incident.

The translation of *Elio, Eloi, lama sabachthani?* is more complicated than is usually recorded in the King James version of the Gospels. More accurately, the translation is *I am, I am, wherefore have You left Me. I am, I am,* brings the quotation close to the Mosaic theophany at Sinai (Mt. Horeb) where God answers *I am the I am* to Moses's question about who He is. This translation better reveals the Judaic insight of God as an abstraction closely related to being.

I suggest that as death approached, Jesus, like Hamlet, understood the finality of death. His call suggests that He lost the sense of preordination and realized fully the nothingness ahead. If we use the *I am* translation, He is fully acknowledging an impending *not to be*. Even more parallel to Hamlet, in the most mystical of the gospels, Jesus's ultimate cry is *It is finished* (John, 19:30). Not surprisingly, as death approaches, Hamlet and Jesus meet in *The rest is silence.*[8,9]

The Gospels relate the death of Jesus as the penultimate event in his ministry. The end is the beginning—He is the alpha and the omega. The Gospels present the well-known events of His Resurrection. Read literally, these events chronicle His appearances to His followers, primarily at the Pentecost, evidencing His corporeal return.

Psychoanalytically, His appearances are a chronicle of the mourning of His death by His followers with their progressive idealization and identification with Him. He is finding His way

---

8 In the *Hamlet Quarto, 1* (1603), Shakespeare draws from Luke and has Hamlet say *Heaven receive my soul*. Without doubt had Shakespeare not revised those final words, Hamlet would be a much less interesting character and *Hamlet* a much less interesting play.
9 As further evidence of Shakespeare's ability to condense meanings, *the rest* has two meanings: *The rest* refers to what will follow; but *the rest* also means a state of repose, the sleep of death.

into their hearts, never to be lost again. His influence continues and grows—a metaphysical life after death. It is an apotheosis. He becomes immortal.

Hamlet, like Jesus, comes to a full realization of death as the end of existence. As an acknowledgement of his sense of finiteness, Hamlet asks Horatio to *tell my story* so that he be remembered.

The paradox is that in accepting finiteness, Hamlet, like Jesus, lives on. Hamlet, as the titular character in one of the greatest dramas in the English language, like Jesus, continues as one of the most discussed characters of all time. If it is true that the mourning of the death of his son, Hamnet, is the underpinning of Shakepseare's writing *Hamlet,* then Shakespeare, through Hamlet, provided his son with everlasting life.

8 Existentialism and Psychosis

As a bold extension of rational positivism that began in the Renaissance and was fully embraced by Western culture in the eighteenth century, Freud (1900) in his psychoanalytic exploration of dreams, neurosis, and psychosis had the hubris to make the irrational rational. Subsequent psychoanalytic understanding of personality development included exposition of ontogenesis, the development of the self. The psychoanalytic study of ontogenesis is essentially a study of the origins and psychodynamics of being. Viewed psychoanalytically, psychosis is a profound disturbance in the development of the self. In the study of being, existentialism and the psychoanalytic study of psychosis meet.

From the rational positivist perspective, hence the psychoanalytic view, most religious–cosmological aspirations regarding personal continuance are believed an elaborate defense against full realization of the end of personal existence. Out of the fear of eventual nothingness, such contentions conjure illusions of continuance (Freud, 1961). [1]

Although having many meanings, existentialism is at base an appreciation of being. As espoused by Martin Heidegger, existentialism emphasizes death, finitude, and nothingness (1927). [2]

---

[1] As a major early dissenter of Freud, Carl G. Jung proposed, "The decisive question for man: Is he related to something infinite or not? Only if we know that the thing which truly matters is the infinite can we avoid fixing our interest on futilities, and upon all kinds of goals which are not of real importance.... The feeling for the infinite, however, can be attained only if we are bounded to the utmost. The greatest limitation for man is the 'self'; it is manifested in the experience, 'I am only that'" (p. 325, 1961). In concert with most religions, Jung provides a defense against the fear of inevitable nonexistence. In contrast, the acceptance of "I am only that" is the acceptance of an essential truth, the essence of being.
[2] Following World War II, the writings of Jean-Paul Sartre (1943) widely popularized Heidegger's existentialist thought.

Psychoanalytically, the self as an integrated, enduring, and consistent sense develops as a result of a sequential developmental unfolding within a propitious environment. Freud conceptualized the interaction as a complementary series: the nature–nurture dyad. This dyad allows for almost infinite possibilities and variations in personality development.

Developmentally the earliest sense of self is a fluid sense of oneness, an "oceanic" absence of differentiation of inner and outer.[3] It is the dawning of awareness. The external, essentially the mother, through empathic attunement to the infant, is initially experienced as under the control of the infant.[4] This omnipotent, egocentric illusionary "other Eden" gradually and reluctantly yields as the demands of the external make themselves known. The beginning differentiation of inside from outside, more specifically the differentiation of self from other, albeit fluid and shifting, marks the beginning of the individual. It is the dawning of responsiveness.

Further development and the concomitantly increasing complexity of internal and external needs couple with the inevitable imperfection in mother–infant attunement to increase the sense of separateness. This sense of separateness is heavily dependent on the internalization of the mothering person as a separate yet integrated concept of other. The internalization, differentiation, and integration frequently are achieved through the vehicle of a thing, an object that becomes endowed with meaning—the transitional object, immortalized by Charles Schulz's cartoon character Linus and his blanket (Winnicott, 1953, 1967). The object is transitional in that psychically it is part mother and part not-mother and part self and part not-self. The appearance of the transitional object marks a developmental achievement that reflects the end of the dyad and the beginning of a recognition of the importance of a third. The infant is developing a complex inner psychical life.[5]

---

[3] Even though Daniel Stern's (1985) research showed that newborn infants, including infants in utero, respond to the environment with differentiations, the psychoanalytic view of ontology reflects the retroactively organized, partially repressed, subjective experience of each individual. This subjective view of ontology, largely held in the unconscious, closely parallels mythic views of the Creation (Oremland, 1989).

[4] Mother is used generically for the interpersonal other who consistently responds to and cares for the infant.

[5] Donald Winnicott (1953, 1967, 1971) championed the idea that the transitional object morphs into a metaphoric psychic space that is, to use his poetic language, "the me and the not-me," in which he "locates" the dream, creativity, and cultural experiences.

Depending on the degree of frustration, affects (emotions) play a major role in the developmental sequence.[6] The differentiated self and other representations are invested early with affects of varying intensity. These affect-laden representations are experienced as polarized concepts, all good or all bad, until repressive capacities develop that allow resolution of affective and conceptual inconsistencies. Only then are the self and other concepts harmonized and integrated as an integrated coalesced self. With integration of the self and other representations, a sense of self-cohesion develops. With self-cohesion and integration, a sense of being, come the capacity for interpersonal relatedness, intimacy, and transcendence.

The sense of being is achieved by sublimations and repressions of conceptual inconsistencies and excessive affects invested in anachronistic and atavistic concepts of self and other. The specific contents and affective components of the sublimations and repressions regarding the self and other concepts provide the overarching emotional intonation to the sense of being.

Viewed psychoanalytically, schizophrenic psychosis is a severe disturbance of self-cohesion. Subjectively, it is marked by a fleeting or continuing sense of emptiness and inauthenticity with fear of self-fragmentation, self-disintegration, and existential anxiety.[7] During severe regressive psychotic episodes, ontogenetic regression, as repressive ability is lost, anachronistic and atavistic self states are re-experienced. Infantile concepts of self and other are again endowed with primitive affects and polarized into good and bad and/or experienced as unmitigatedly destructive, alien, and threatening. With increased de-differentiation of inner and outer, the external world becomes terror-filled as infantile rage is projected onto and seen as coming from others. The individuals on whom this rage is projected may be furiously attacked in a delusional flurry of self-defense. Panic, lashing out, paranoia, and catatonic excitement or catatonic paralysis frequently ensue.

---

6 Intensity of affect is relative to the fragility of the developing intrapsychic structures that contain and defend against it and the degree of inevitable and avoidable frustrations.
7 Existential anxiety is distinguished from neurotic anxiety in that existential anxiety is a cataclysmic anxiety, the fear of the collapse of the self and the experience of utter nothingness (Sartre, 1943). Neurotic anxiety is a mixture of fear of loss of love and protection and guilt.

The onset of the regressive fragmentation and dissolution of the self can be insidiously progressive or suddenly dramatic. Such regressions are precipitated by events. Although the importance of the events may be major and apparent, more often they are idiosyncratic to the individual and reflect early and specific interpersonal vulnerabilities.

HAMLET AND EXISTENTIALISM

In *Hamlet* the precipitating event of Hamlet's mental demise is his mind-shattering realization that his mother is deceitful and untrustworthy—a primal disillusionment. He comes to realize that she *seems* more than *is*. As subtext to this realization is the probability of his father's murder and that his mother may have been an accomplice. No one is more clear, more concise, or more accurate than Gertrude when describing the propitiating events leading to Hamlet's psychosis.[8]

> **Queen:** *I doubt it is no other but the main,*
> *His father's death and our o'er-hasty marriage.*
> (Act II, Sc. ii, lines 56–57)

Yet, the point is not whether Hamlet is psychotic, as is usually argued, but how does his psychosis make the play into a masterpiece. I suggest that because of Shakespeare's intuitive understanding of psychosis, he through Hamlet makes visible the excruciatingly terrifying fear of nonexistence. Through experiencing threatened nonexistence, Hamlet comes to a new understanding of life and death. Life and death are the polarized abstractions of being and not being.

The moment of experiencing nonexistence is graphically presented in Hamlet's catatonic excitement following the appearance of the ghost in Act I. Horatio best describes the highly jangled thoughts and actions of his friend as he attempts to quiet the frantic Hamlet on the parapet.

> **Horatio:** *These are but wild and whirling words, my lord.*
> (Act I, Sc. v, line 139)

---

[8] Evaluating Hamlet in this way assumes that he is a physical person with a developmental history and specific vulnerabilities rather than a created character conceived for dramatic and theatrical effects.

The moment of beginning reintegration is epitomized in Hamlet's one-word response to Claudius, as he accepts the inevitability of banishment (being forcibly removed from his conflict).

Hamlet: *For England?*
King: *Ay, Hamlet.*
Hamlet: *Good.*
(Act IV, Sc. iii, lines 47–49)

The play captivates us for in it we can follow a journey, a journey we are afraid to undertake. With Hamlet we experience fear of death and we experience death's being mastered by an acceptance of death as not being. With Hamlet, vicariously and fleetingly, we transcend fear of death by understanding death. As L.C. Knights (1960) accurately identified in *Hamlet,* ". . . the meditation on death is no mere brooding" (p. 232). Like Knights we are endlessly fascinated by Hamlet's "energetic and transforming assimilation of the basic facts of the human condition" (p. 232)—that the essence of living is being and that without being life is an empty nothingness.

Shakespeare stuns us when his titular character in a moment of utter aloneness and great travail asks the quintessential existential question,

Hamlet: *To be, or not to be, . . .*
(Act III, Sc. i, line 56)

and when on facing death utters the quintessential existential answer,

Hamlet: *. . . —the rest is silence.*
(Act V, Sc. ii, line 363)

The succinctness of Shakespeare's understanding of the essence of humanness continues the existential tradition, a tradition that long anticipated Heidegger and Sartre. This existential tradition was given voice on Mt. Sinai when God revealed himself to Moses as *"I am the I am";* returned in the Cartesian, *"I think therefore I am";* and changed twentieth-century thought when Albert Einstein reduced matter to nothing more than energy, $E=MC^2$.

References

Bergmann, M. S. (1992). *In the Shadow of Moloch: The Sacrifice of Children and Its Impact on Western Religions*. New York: Columbia University Press.

Brandes, G. (1963). *William Shakespeare: A Critical Study. Vol. II*. New York: Frederick Ungar.

Bright, T. (1586). *Treatise of Melancholie*. New York: Facsimile Text Society, 1940.

Campbell, L. B. (1930). *Shakespeare's Tragic Heroes: Slaves of Passion*. Cambridge, England: Cambridge University Press.

Deutsch, H. (1942). Some forms of emotional disturbance and their relationship to schizophrenia. *Psychoanal. Q.*, 11:301–321.

Eissler, K. R. (1971). *Discourse on Hamlet and* Hamlet. New York: International Universities Press.

Eliot. T. S. (1920). Hamlet and his problem. In: *The Sacred Wood*, ed. S. Wellman. New York: Barnes & Noble, 1966.

Empson, W. (1947). *Seven Types of Ambiguity*. New York: New Directions.

Fisch. H. (1971). *Hamlet and the Word*. New York: Frederick Ungar.

Freud, A. (1936). *The Ego and the Mechanisms of Defense*. New York: International Universities Press, 1966.

Freud, S. (1897–1902). *The Origins of Psychoanalysis*. New York: Basic Books, 1954.

———. (1900). The Interpretation of Dreams. *Standard Edition*, 4 & 5. London: Hogarth Press, 1953.

_____. (1910). Leonardo da Vinci and a memory of his childhood. *Standard Edition*, 11:59–137. London: Hogarth Press, 1957.

_____. (1914). The Moses of Michelangelo. *Standard Edition*, 13: 209–236. London: Hogarth Press, 1955.

_____. (1917). Mourning and melancholia. *Standard Edition*, 14: 237–258. London: Hogarth Press, 1957.

_____. (1927). The future of an illusion. *Standard Edition*, 21:5–56. London: Hogarth Press, 1961.

_____. (1937). Letter to Percy Allen. In the possession of the author.

Gedo, J. (1983). *Portraits of the Artist*. New York: Guilford.

Gedo, M. (1980). *Picasso: Art as Autobiography*. Chicago: University of Chicago Press.

Goethe, J. W. (1785). Wilhelm Meister's Apprentice. In: *Hamlet: Enter Critic*, eds. C. Sacks and E. Whan. New York: Appleton–Century–Crofts, 1960.

Greenacre, P. (1957). The childhood of the artist. *The Psychoanalytic Study of the Child*, 12:47–72. New York: International Universities Press.

Harbage, A. (1947). As they liked it: an essay on Shakespeare and mortality. In: *Hamlet: Enter Critic*, eds. C. Sacks and E. Whan. New York: Appleton–Century–Crofts, 1960.

Hazlitt, W. (1817). Character of Shakespeare's plays: *Hamlet*. In: *Hamlet*, ed. C. Hoy. New York: Norton, 1963.

Heidegger, M. (1927). *Being and Time*, trans. J. Macquarrie and E. Robinson. New York: Harper, 1982.

Internet Shakespeare. *Hamlet Folio, 1*. Vol. II, 1623.

Internet Shakespeare. *Hamlet Quarto, 1*. 1603.

Jones, E. (1949). *Hamlet and Oedipus*. New York: Norton.

Jung, C. G. (1961). *Memories, Dreams, Reflections*. New York: Pantheon.

REFERENCES

Kernberg, O. (1975). *Borderline Conditions and Pathological Narcissism.* New York: Aronson.

Knights, L. C. (1960). *Some Shakespearean Themes and an Approach to Hamlet.* Stanford, Calif.: Stanford University Press.

Kris, E. (1952). *Psychoanalytic Explorations in Art.* New York: International Universities Press.

Levin, H. (1959). *The Question of Hamlet.* New York: Oxford University Press.

Lewis, C. S. (1942). Hamlet: The prince or the poem. In: *Hamlet*, ed. C. Hoy. New York: Norton, 1963.

Liebert, R. S. (1982). *Michelangelo.* New Haven, Conn.: Yale University Press.

Oremland, J. D. (1980). Mourning and its effect on Michelangelo's art. *Ann. Psychoanal.*, 8:317–351. New York: International Universities Press.

————. (1981). The wide scope of psychoanalytic investigations of art. *Dialogue*, 5:3–13.

————. (1983). Death and transformation in *Hamlet. Psychoanal. Inq.*, 3:485–512. Hillsdale, N.J.: The Analytic Press.

————. (1984). Empathy and its relation to the appreciation of the formative arts, painting and sculpture. In: *Empathy I*, eds. J. Lichtenberg et al. Hillsdale, N.J.: The Analytic Press.

————. (1989). *Michelangelo's Sistine Ceiling: A Psychoanalytic Study of Creativity.* Madison, Conn.: International Universities Press.

————. (1997). *The Origins and Psychodynamics of Creativity: A Psychoanalytic Perspective.* Madison, Conn.: International Universities Press.

Pollock, G. H. (1975). Mourning and memoralization through music. *Ann. Psychoanal.*, 3:423–436. New York: International Universities Press.

Prosser, E. (1971). *Hamlet and Revenge.* Stanford, Calif.: Stanford University Press.

Rose, G. J. (1980). *The Power of Form.* New York: International Universities Press.

Rowse, A. L. (1963). *William Shakespeare, a Biography.* New York: Harper and Row.

Santayana, G. (1900). *Interpretations of Poetry and Religion.* New York: Charles Scribner and Sons, 1969.

Sartre, J.-P. (1943). *Being and Nothingness: An Essay on Phenomenological Ontology,* trans. H. E. Barnes. New York: Philosophical Library, 1956.

Stern, D. (1985). *The Interpersonal World of the Infant: A View from Psychoanalysis and Developmental Psychology.* New York: Basic Books.

Summers, M. (1926). *The History of Witchcraft and Demonology.* London: Routledge & Kegan Paul, 1965.

Washburn College (1980). *Holy Bible.* New York: Oxford University Press.

Wilson, J. D. (1970). *What Happens in* Hamlet. Cambridge, England: Cambridge University Press.

Winnicott, D. (1953). Transitional objects and transitional phenomena. *Int. J. Psycho-anal.,* 34:89–97.

_____. (1967). The location of the cultural experience. *Int. J. Psycho-anal.,* 48:368–373.

_____. (1971). *Playing and Reality.* New York: Basic Books.

ANNOTATED STUDIES CONSULTED

Hoy, C. (ed.) (1963). *Hamlet.* New York: Norton.

Jenkins, H. (2002). *Hamlet.* London: Methuen & Co.

Rowse, A. L. (ed.) (1978). *The Annotated Shakespeare, III.* New York: Clarkson N. Potter.

Line Index[1]

ACT I SCENE II
LINES 68-76
Queen: *Good Hamlet, cast thy nighted colour off,* 24, 27, 35
LINES 83-84
Hamlet: *These indeed seem,* 25
LINES 106-112
King: *We pray you throw to earth this unprevailing woe,* 20
LINES 118-119
Queen: *Let not thy mother lose her prayers, Hamlet,* 27
LINES 129-134
Hamlet: *O that this too too sullied flesh would melt,* viii, 97
LINES 138-142; 186-188; 240-242
Hamlet: *But two months dead—nay, not so much, not two—,* 9
LINES 176-179
Horatio: *My lord, I came to see your father's funeral,* 24

SCENE V
LINES 23-25
Ghost: *If thou didst ever thy dear father love—,* 12
LINES 29-31; 34-40
Hamlet: *Haste me to know't, that I with wings as swift,* 53
LINES 41-46
Hamlet: *O my prophetic soul! My uncle!,* 53
LINES 43-46
Ghost: *With witchcraft of his wit, with traitorous gifts,* 25

---

[1] Line references are from William Shakespeare, *Hamlet*, The Arden Edition, ed. by Harold Jenkins (London: Thomson, 2002).

LINES 74-75
Ghost: *Thus was I, sleeping, by a brother's hand,* 30
LINES 81-83
Ghost: *If thou has nature in thee, bear it not,* 12
LINES 84-86
Ghost: *But howsomever thou pursuest this act,* 13–14
LINE 91
Ghost: *Remember me,* 7
LINES 102-103
Hamlet: *And thy commandment all alone shall live,* 13, 93
LINES 105-110
Hamlet: *O most pernicious woman!,* 54, 55
LINE 139
Horatio: *These are but wild and whirling words, my lord,* 55, 114
LINE 144
Hamlet: *It is an honest ghost, that let me tell you,* 55
LINES 148-149
Hamlet: *Give me one poor request,* 56
LINES 158-160
Hamlet: *Ah ha, boy, say'st thou so? Art thou there, truepenny?,* 56
LINE 164
Hamlet: *Hic et ubique?,* 56
LINES 170-172
Hamlet: *Well said, old mole. Canst work i'th' earth so fast?,* 56
LINES 174-175
Hamlet: *There are more things in heaven and earth, Horatio,* 39, 57
LINES 177-180
Hamlet: *Here, as before, never, so help you mercy,* 57
LINES 196-197
Hamlet: *The time is out of joint,* 93

ACT II SCENE I
LINES 75-84; 87-100
Ophelia: *O my lord, my lord, I have been so affrighted,* 58–59

LINE INDEX

SCENE II
LINES 19-26
Queen: *Good gentlemen, he hath much talk'd of you,* 26
LINES 54-57
King: *He tells me, my dear Gertrude, he hath found,* 26, 86, 114
LINE 167
King: *We will try it,* 26
LINES 208-211
Polonius: *How pregnant sometimes his replies are—,* 60
LINES 213-217
Polonius: *My lord, I will take my leave of you,* 60
LINES 224-226
Hamlet: *My excellent good friends. How dost thou,* 60
LINES 269-270
Hamlet: *But in the beaten way of friendship,* 60–61
LINE 275
Hamlet: *Come, come, deal justly with me,* 61
LINES 278-281; 287-288
Hamlet: *Anything but to th' purpose. You were sent for,* 61
LINES 292-317
Guildenstern: *My lord, we were sent for,* 61–63
LINES 366-375
Hamlet: *Gentlemen, you are welcome to Elsinore,* 63–64
LINES 538-539
Hamlet: *Very well.* (To all the Players) *Follow that lord, and look you mock him not,* 64
LINES 543-573
Hamlet: *O what a rouge and peasant slave am I!,* 64–65
LINES 593-601
Hamlet: *If a do blench, I know my course,* 65

ACT III SCENE I
LINE 37
Gertrude: *I shall obey you,* 26

LINES 46-49
Polonius: *We are oft to blame in this,* 15, 66
LINES 49-54
King: *O 'tis too true. How smart a lash that speech doth give me conscience,* 15, 66
LINES 56-90
Hamlet: *To be, or not to be,* viii, 24, 66, 80, 98, 108, 115
LINE 83
Hamlet: *Thus conscience does make cowards of us all,* 12
LINES 88-90; 92-108; 111-120
Hamlet: *Soft you now, the fair Ophelia!,* 66, 83, 84–5
LINES 122-130
Hamlet: *I am myself indifferent honest,* 85
LINES 129-130
Hamlet: *We are arrant knaves all, believe none of us,* 67
LINES 135
Ophelia: *O help him, you sweet heavens,* 67
LINES 136-142
Hamlet: *If thou dost marry, I'll give thee this plague for thy dowry,* 85
LINES 143-152; 159-163
Ophelia: *Heavenly powers, restore him,* 76, 86
LINES 164-166
King: *Love? His affections do not that way tend,* 68
LINE 190
King: *Madness in great ones must not unwatch'd go,* 68

SCENE II
LINES 65-74
Hamlet: *For thou hast been as one, in suff'ring all,* 68–69
LINES 80-84
Hamlet: *If his occulted guilt do not itself unkennel in one speech,* 69
LINE 107
Queen: *Come hither, my dear Hamlet, sit by me,* 27, 30
LINES 124-133
Hamlet: *For look you how cheerfully my mother looks and my father died,* 69

LINE INDEX

LINE 143
Ophelia: *You are naught*, 69
LINE 225
Queen: *The lady doth protest too much, methinks*, 27
LINES 232-239; 255-258
Hamlet: The Mousetrap—*marry, how tropically!*, 70
LINES 280-281
Hamlet: *O good Horatio, I'll take the ghost's word for a thousand pound*, 71
LINES 300-301
Guildenstern: *Good my lord, put your discourse into some frame*, 71
LINE 348
Hamlet: *It is as easy as lying*, 71
LINES 361-363
Hamlet: *Call me what instrument you will*, 71
LINES 379-390
Hamlet: *'Tis now the very witching time of night*, 72

SCENE III
LINES 1-4
King: *I like him not, nor stands it safe with us*, 18
LINES 36-38
King: *O, my offence is rank, it smells to heaven*, 15, 21, 95
LINES 51-55
King: *But O, what form of prayer can serve my turn?*, 16, 21
LINES 57-60
King: *In the corrupted currents of this world*, 16
LINES 61-64
King: *There is no shuffling, there the action lies in his true nature*, 16
LINES 69-72
King: *Help, angels! Make assay*, 16
LINES 73-78
Hamlet: *Now might I do it pat, now a is a-praying*, 14
LINES 97-98
King: *My words fly up, my thoughts remain below*, 14

SCENE IV

LINES 8-15
Queen: *Hamlet, thou has thy father much offended,* 28
LINES 17-19
Hamlet: *Come, come, and sit you down, you shall not budge,* 25
LINES 20-21
Queen: *What wilt thou do?,* 29
LINES 28-30
Hamlet: *A bloody deed. Almost as bad, good mother,* 29, 72
LINES 34-38
Hamlet: *Peace, sit you down, and let me wring your heart; for so I shall,* 29, 72
LINES 54-63
Hamlet: *Look here upon this picture, and on this,* 10
LINES 63-65; 76-79
Hamlet: *This was your husband. Look you now what follows,* 73
LINES 88-94
Queen: *O Hamlet, speak no more,* 73, 30
LINES 91-94
Hamlet: *Nay, but to live in the rank sweat of an enseamed bed,* 73
LINES 96-99
Hamlet: *A murderer and a villain, a slave that is not twentieth part the tithe,* 73
LINE 102
Queen: *No more,* 74, 75
LINES 106-114
Queen: *Alas, he's mad,* 31, 74
LINES 113-115
Ghost: *O step between her and her fighting soul,* 31
LINES 117-118
Queen: *That you do bend your eye on vacancy,* 74
LINES 122-125; 131-135; 139-148
Queen: *This is the very coinage of your brain,* 75
LINES 151-154
Hamlet: *Confess yourself to heaven,* 76

LINE INDEX

LINE 158
Queen: *O Hamlet, thou has cleft my heart in twain,* 76
LINES 161-162; 183-201
Hamlet: *But go not to my uncle's bed,* 31, 76, 77
LINES 199-201
Queen: *Be thou assur'd, if words be made of breath,* 32
LINES 213-219
Hamlet: *This man shall set me packing,* 32, 77

ACT IV SCENE I
LINES 7-13
Queen: *Mad as the sea and wind when both contend,* 17, 32, 78
LINES 12-15
King: *O heavy deed! It had been so with us had we been there,* 17, 32

SCENE II
LINES 10-20
Hamlet: *That I can keep your counsel and not mine own,* 78

SCENE III
LINES 16-25
King: *Now, Hamlet, where's Polonius?,* 78, 79, 80
LINE 49
Hamlet: *Good,* 80, 81
LINES 51-56
Hamlet: *But come, for England. Farewell, dear mother,* 80, 106
LINES 67-71
King: *By letters congruing to that effect, the present death of Hamlet,* 80–81

SCENE IV
LINES 13-14
Hamlet: *Who commands them, sir?,* 44
LINES 18-20
Captain: *We go to gain a little patch of ground,* 45

LINES 32-44
Hamlet: *How all occasions do inform against me,* 45
LINES 45-50
Hamlet: *Sith I have cause, and will, and strength, and means,* 12, 49–50
LINES 59-66
Hamlet: *I see the imminent death of twenty thousand men,* 46

SCENE V
LINE 1
Queen: *I will not speak with her,* 33
LINES 4-7
A gentleman (to the queen): *She speaks much of her father,* 87
LINES 14-15
Horatio: *'Twere good she were spoke with, for she may strew,* 33
LINES 17-20
Queen: *To my sick soul, as sin's true nature is,* 33
LINES 29-32
Ophelia (sings): *He is dead and gone, lady?,* 87
LINES 41-44
King: *How do you, pretty lady,* 88
LINES 52-55; 60-63
Ophelia (sings): *Then up he rose, and donn'd his clo'es,* 88
LINES 72-73
Ophelia: *Good night, ladies, good night. Sweet ladies, good night,* 88
LINES 159-160
Laertes: *O heavens, is't possible a young maid's wits,* 88
LINES 178-179
Ophelia: *There's rue for you,* 89
LINES 181-183
Ophelia: *I would give you some violets,* 89
LINES 187-197
Ophelia (sings): *And will a not come again?,* 89–90

SCENE VII
LINES 4-5
King: *That he which hath your noble father slain,* 18

LINE INDEX

LINES 9-18
King: *O, for two special reasons, which may to you perhaps seem much,* 28
LINES 54-58
Laertes: *It warms the very sickness in my heart,* 18–19
LINES 62-69; 106-108
King: *I will work him to an exploit,* 19
LINES 109-122
King: *Not that I think you did not love your father,* 17
LINES 123-127
King: *Hamlet comes back; what would you undertake,* 19
LINE 162
Queen: *One woe doth tread upon another's heel,* 33
LINES 172-182
Queen: *Clamb'ring to hang, an envious sliver broke,* 90

ACT V SCENE I
LINES 23-31
Gravedigger 2: *If this had not been a gentlewoman,* 94
LINES 75-79
Hamlet: *How the knave jowls it to th' ground, as if 'twere,* 95
LINES 138-144; 156-157
Hamlet: *How long has thou been a grave-maker?,* 96
LINES 191-192
Hamlet: *Dost thou think Alexander looked o' this fashion,* 96
LINES 196-198; 201-209
Hamlet: *Alexander died, Alexander was buried, Alexander returneth to dust,* 97
LINES 222-224; 233-235; 290-292
Priest: *She should in ground unsanctified been lodg'd,* 99
LINES 236-239
Queen: *Sweets to the sweet. Farewell,* 34
LINES 253-256
Hamlet: *I prithee take thy fingers from my throat,* 99
LINES 268; 280-283
Queen: *For love of God forbear him,* 34

SCENE II
LINES 4-5
Hamlet: *Sir, in my heart there was a kind of fighting*, 100
LINES 9-11
Hamlet: *And that should learn us there's a divinity that shapes our ends*, 100
LINE 25
Hamlet: *My head should be struck off*, 42
LINES 47-49
Horatio: *How was this seal'd?*, 42
LINES 56-58
Horatio: *So Guildenstern and Rosencrantz go to't*, 42-43
LINE 62
Horatio: *Why, what a kings is this!*, 43
LINES 64-70
Hamlet: *He that hath kill'd my king and whor'd my mother*, 49
LINES 100-102
Osric: *My lord, his Majesty bade me signify to you that a has laid a great wager on your head*, 103
LINES 173-175
Hamlet: *I will win for him and I can*, 100
LINES 206-207
Hamlet: *I have been in continual practice*, 100, 102
LINES 208-209; 211-220
Hamlet: *Thou wouldst not think how ill all's here about my heart*, 101
LINES 215-216
Hamlet: *Not a whit. We defy augury*, 39
LINES 246-248
Laertes: *But till that time I do receive your offer'd love like love*, 102
LINES 252-254
Hamlet: *I'll be your foil, Laertes*, 103
LINES 290-292
Queen: *He's fat and scant of breath*, 34
LINE 300
Laertes (aside): *And yet it is almost against my conscience*, 104

LINE INDEX

LINE 302
Hamlet: *I pray you pass with your best violence*, 105
LINES 312-313
Laertes: *Why, as a woodcock to mine own springe, Osric*, 38
LINES 315-316
Queen: *O my dear Hamlet! The drink*, 30, 34
LINES 319-326
Laertes: *It is here, Hamlet. Hamlet, thou art slain*, 105
LINE 326
Laertes: *The King—the King's to blame*, 38
LINE 329
King: *O yet defend me, friends. I am but hurt*, 20
LINE 332
Hamlet: *Follow my mother*, 20, 106
LINES 334-336
Laertes: *Exchange forgiveness with me, noble Hamlet*, 38
LINE 338
Hamlet: *Heaven make thee free of it*, 106
LINES 341-342
Hamlet: *As this fell sergeant, Death*, 106
LINE 344
Hamlet: *Report me and my cause aright*, 106
LINE 346
Horatio: *I am more an antique Roman than a Dane*, 39–43, 107
LINES 351-354
Hamlet: *If thou didst ever hold me in thy heart*, 43–44, 107
LINES 360-361
Hamlet: *But I do prophesy th'election lights*, 44, 50, 107
LINE 363
Hamlet: *The rest is silence*, 107, 108, 115
LINES 393-395
Fortinbras: *For me, with sorrow I embrace my fortune*, 50, 104
LINES 401-403
Fortinbras: *Bear Hamlet like a soldier to the stage*, 46

Index

A

a fantasy and trick of fame, 49
abstraction(s), 108, 114
   polarized, 114
acceptance, 80, 107, 111
   of death, 79, 115
   of finiteness of the self, viii
accomplice, 15, 25, 54, 72, 106, 114
accusation(s), 11, 25, 29, 63, 73, 84
   ghost's, 55, 65
   paranoid, 52
acorn, 2
act, 12–13, 14, 21, 57–78, 85
   sinful, 16
Act I, 9–11, 35, 97, 114
Act II, 64
Act III, 9, 11, 27, 55, 64, 66
Act IV, 40, 49, 81
Act V, 20, 30, 42, 80, 93, 100
Adam, 94–95, 104
admonition, 12–13, 76
advisor, esteemed, 1, 58
affect(s) (emotions), 4, 37, 51–52, 59–60, 62, 65, 83, 97, 111
   disturbance in, 51
   primitive, 113
affection(ate), 23, 30, 38, 66, 83
afterlife (life after death), 10, 47, 90–91, 98, 100
Age
   Elizabethan, 39
   New, 64, 94, 104

aggressor, identification with the, 41, 47
agony, 86
aimlessness, 49
all that lives must die, 35
Allen, P., 7
aloneness, utter, 115
alpha, 108
altruism, 40, 41–42
ambiguity (ambiguities), 4, 7
ambivalence, 41, 71, 74, 106
American Conservatory Theater, San Francisco, 5
analogy (analogies), 52
   between creating and dreaming, 4
analysis, dream, 6
And thy commandment all alone, 13, 93
Angel, Blue, The, 41
anger, 49, 55, 64, 81, 85–86
answer, 19, 61, 79, 96, 108
   existential, 115
anxiety, 47, 62, 75
   cataclysmic, 113
   existential, vii, 52, 113
   neurotic, 113
apology (apologies), 38
apotheosis, 109
apparition, 10
appearances, 25, 33, 44, 108, 112
   ghost, 9, 114
appreciation, art, 5
arc of the play, viii
arcane, 46, 47, 91
archetypical, the, 6, 7

army (Fortinbras's), 44, 49, 81
arras, 12, 29
art, vii, 2–6, 95
art work, 2–7
   the anatomy of, 6
   the psychoanalytic study of, 2
as if personality, 24
aspirations, 47
   religious–cosmological, 111
assimilation, transforming, 115
associations
   dreamer's, 6
   loose, 59
attunement, empathic, 112
audience(s), 5, 11, 38, 55–56
awareness, viii, 31, 97
   dawning of, 112

B

bait, human, 83
banishment, 79, 81, 115
bed, mother's, 31, 57, 73, 76
bed chamber (mother's, queen's, Gertrude's) (*See also:* Scene, Closet), 10, 57, 71–72, 81–82
behavior, erratic, 55–56, 58
being, 1, 98, 101, 108, 113–115
   essence of, 53, 111
   sense of, viii, 113
   state(s) of, viii, 66
Bergmann, M., 48, 103
Bernardo, 10
betrayal(s), 55, 61, 85–86, 89
biography
   psychoanalytic, 3
Blithe Spirit, 11
block, executioner's, 7
Blots, Rorschach Ink, 4
Brandes, G., 58, 83
Bright, T., 11
brother, 1, 11, 21, 41, 70, 90, 93

C

Caesar, J., 64, 83, 97

Cain and Abel, 20, 21, 95
Campbell, L., 11
Cartesian (Descartes), 115
cathexsis, 62
Catholicism, medieval, 99
centurion, 104
challenge(s), 19, 39
character, titular (*See also:* Hamlet), 1, 109, 115
Christ, Passion of (*See:* Passion Play)
Church, Catholic, 40, 94
Claudius, 2, 9, 11–21, 23, 26–34, 37, 42–43, 49, 54–55, 58, 64, 68–73, 77–81, 83, 87–89, 94–95, 100, 102–103, 105–106, 115
   the end of, 20
climax (of the play), 20
commandment, 13, 93, 105
commission, 6, 42
communicating, conscious and unconscious, 7
Complex, Oedipal, 2, 27, 31, 53
complicity, 26, 29
Comte, A., 42
concealment, 85
condensation(s), 4, 5, 7, 60, 93
   psychotic, 80
condonement, vicarious (unconscious), 103
confession, 10, 30, 38, 85
conflict, 2, 12, 17, 70, 100, 115
confrontation, viii, 1, 2, 81
   Hamlet–Gertrude, 25, 29, 86
   humankind's, 21
   Laertes–Hamlet, 34, 38
   with death, 93
conscience, 2, 12, 35, 74
continuance, 7, 13, 20, 44, 46–49, 91, 98, 104, 107, 111
continuity
   cultural, 48
   personal, 48, 52
   sense of, 52
contrition, 10, 14, 16
corruptibility (Horatio), 33
corruption, 93

INDEX

counterpoint, 44, 50
   philosophic, 39
court (*See also:* Elsinore), 15, 23, 33, 58, 68, 69, 104
covenant, 93
Coward, N., 11
cracked pot, 52
Creation, mythic view of, 112
creativity, 1–4, 6, 7, 112
critic(s), 5, 14, 23
Cross, The, 107
   Fourteen Stations of, 104
   Legend of, 95
crow, cock, 11
Crucifixion, The, 21, 95
culture(s), 7, 48
   Western, 2, 111
cup, poisoned, 107
cycle, revenge, 105

D

da Vinci, L., 3
dagger, 100
daughter, 64
De Vere, E., 7
death, 13, 15, 18, 20–23, 32–33, 35, 37, 43–44, 48–50, 54, 78–79, 86–88, 90–94, 96–101, 107–109, 111, 114
   and mourning, vii, 3
   acceptance of, 79, 115
   Angel of, 103–104, 107
   confrontation with, 1, 93, 96
   denial of, 48, 50
   doubtful, 90
   existential view of, 81, 98
   exploration of, 7
   fear of, vii, 1, 48, 104, 115
   finiteness of, viii, 48, 98
   Hamlet, of, 39, 44, 68, 93–94, 103–104
   immutability of, 106
   living, 1
   messenger of, 100
   Ophelia's, 33, 88, 94
   preordained, 81
   responses to, vii–viii
   senseless, 32
   sleep of, 108
   wish for, viii
decathexsis, 62, 65
deceitfulness, 61
deception, 55, 66–67, 85, 86
deceptiveness, 72
de-differentiation of inner and outer, 113
defense(s) (ego), viii, 40, 48, 62, 87, 90, 111
delay, 12, 14, 37, 70, 89
delusions, 47, 113
demons, 11
Denmark, 18, 44, 81
   King of (*See:* Claudius; King Hamlet)
   Prince of (*See:* Hamlet)
denunciation, 28–29, 67, 69, 71
depression, 51, 53, 62, 64
despair, 81
destiny, viii
Deutsch, H., 24
development, 47, 52–53
   character, 2
   development, human, 6
   personality, 2, 48, 111–112
deviousness, 18
dialecticians, 94
dialogue(s), viii, 6, 10, 15
diatribe, 31
Dietrich, M., 41
differentiation, 48, 52
   inside and outside, 112
   «oceanic», absence of, 112
   of self and other, 55, 112
dilemma, 12–13
disillusionment, primal, 55, 114
disposition, antic, 55, 57–58, 69, 87
ditty, silly, 94, 97
double (Hamlet's), 44
doubt(s) (doubtful), 55, 63–65, 69, 85, 90, 100–102
dove, 48
drama(tization), vii, 4, 43, 50, 53, 62, 83, 88, 93, 109

high, 25
dream(s), 2–7, 12, 13, 46, 93, 111–112
   smoke, 4
duel, 34, 100–104
duplicity, 55
dyad
   Gertrude–Hamlet, 55
   Hamlet–Fortinbras, vii, 44, 50
   Horatio–Hamlet, 39, 40, 57
   mother–son, 31, 54
   nature–nurture, 112
   sadomasochism, 41
dynamics, intrapsychic, 52

E

$E = MC^2$, 115
ego (*See also:* defense[s]), 39, 40, 48
Ego and the Mechanisms of Defense, The, 40
Eden, other, 112
Einstein, A., 115
Eissler, K., 3, 23
elements
   humanizing, 48
   transmissionable of being human, 48
Eliot, T., 102
Eloi, Eloi lama . . . , 108
Elsinore, 18, 27, 33, 42–43, 70, 83
Empson, W., 4
emptiness, feelings of, 52, 113
England, 18, 42, 77, 80
   Elizabethan, 10, 39, 94
   medieval, 7
enigma, 23
Enlightenment, the, 2, 51
envy, 21
episodes, psychotic, 113
epoch(s), 7, 64
essence
   of being, 53, 111
   of humanness, 115
   of identification, 41
   of living, 115
   of man, 62
   of nonexistence, 98

eternity, 98
Eucharist, the, 48
Eve, 104
event
   penultimate, 108
   precipitating, 114
Everlasting, anthropomorphic, 97
evilness, 17, 43
evocation, 7, 16
excitement, catatonic, 113, 114
existence, viii, 62, 109, 111
existential(ism) (existentialist), vii, 1, 16, 52, 81, 96, 98, 107, 111, 113–115
experience(s), vii, viii, 5, 10, 11, 47–48, 62, 74, 111–113, 115
   atavistic, 47, 58
   cultural, 112
   epiphanic, 47
expression, metaphoric, 46
eye for an eye, 13

F

family
   Polonius's, 38
   primal, 21
   royal, 21, 38
fantasies, 12, 49, 86, 91
farewell
   to Claudius, 20
   to (Hamlet's) mother, 106
   ultimate, 20
father, 1–3, 7, 18, 21, 29, 31, 37–38, 40–41, 44, 49–50, 53–54, 80–81, 83, 86, 88–91, 93–94, 102, 114, 108
   incorporeal, 93
   lost, vii, 46, 49
Father into Thy hands I commend, 108
fear(s), 1–2, 29, 37–38, 52, 86, 101, 111–113
   of death, vii, 1, 48, 104, 115
   of finiteness (*See also:* finiteness), 7, 20, 37, 48, 90, 91
   of nonexistence, vii, viii, 114
   unconscious, 2

INDEX

finiteness (finitude), 21, 50, 80, 96, 98–99, 109, 111
   corporeal, 44
   denial of, 48
   fear of, 7, 20, 37, 48, 90, 91
   of death, viii, 98
   of the self, viii
Fisch, H., 93
Fleiss, W., 2
Flight into Egypt, the, 20
flower(s), 40, 88, 89
foil, 19, 37, 94
Folio, first, 96
fool, 94
foreordination, 42, 100
foreshadowings, 64
foretell (foreteller) (foretelling), 64, 101, 103
forgiveness, 20, 38, 102, 106
formation
   character, 24
   cloud, 4
   compromise, 87
   dream, 4
   reaction, 38
Fortinbras, vii–viii, 9, 44–46, 49–50, 81, 104, 107
foul and pestilent congregation, 62
fragmentation, regressive, 114
Francisco, 10
Freud, A., 40–41, 47
Freud, S., 1–4, 6–7, 12, 27, 46, 49, 53–54, 62, 70, 91, 111–112
fullness, 40, 89
funeral (*See also:* Ophelia), 99
fusion, fear of, 52

G

gain
   primary, 58
   secondary, 58
Gedo, J., 3
Gedo, M., 3
Gertrude (*See also:* mother), 9–11, 15, 18, 20–21, 23–35, 53–57, 58, 67, 69, 71, 73–76, 77, 81, 87, 89, 90, 94, 99–100, 103–106, 114
ghost, viii, 10–13, 25, 27, 30, 53–57, 64–65, 69–71, 74, 89, 93, 97, 114
   atemporal (psychological), 11
   medieval, 11
glorification
   medieval, 62
   Renaissance, 62
goals, 41, 111
   self-serving, 16
God, 15–16, 62, 98, 108, 115
Goethe, J., 1–2, 12, 52
Gonzago, the duke, 70
good, 81
Gospel, the, 108
grace, state of, 14, 16
grave (*See also:* Scene, Graveyard), 11, 37, 98–99
   Ophelia's, 10, 99
grave side (*See also:* Ophelia), 10
gravediggers, 94–96
graveyard (*See:* Scene, Graveyard)
Greenacre, P., 3
grief, 32–33
Guildenstern (*See also:* Rosencrantz), 42, 60–61, 63–64, 71, 78
guilt, 2, 15–16, 25, 33, 35, 55, 66, 105, 113

H

hallucination(s), 9, 11, 30, 47, 56, 74
Hamlet, vii, 1–2, 10–15, 17–20, 23–32, 34, 37–39, 42–46, 53–64, 66–79, 80–81, 85–87, 89, 93–109, 114–115
   age of, 44, 96
   and death, viii, 1, 44, 68, 79, 81, 93–94, 97–98, 103–104, 115
   and delay, 12, 37, 89
   and foreordination, 42, 93, 101, 103
   and Fortinbras, 9, 44–46, 49, 56, 107
   and ghost, 10, 11
   and hallucination, 9, 56, 74
   and Jesus, viii
   and letter from, 18

and Oedipus, 2
and primal disillusionment, 114
and psychosis, viii, 31, 32, 42, 53–60, 67–68, 71, 75–76, 79, 84, 87, 114
and revenge, 5, 12, 20
and task (*See also:* task), 11, 12
as rationalist, 39, 57, 107
reintegration of, 50, 81
Hamlet, vii, viii, 1–3, 5, 7, 9–10, 13, 23, 50, 53, 58, 62, 64, 93, 96, 107–109, 114–115
Hamlet Quarto I, 108
Hamnet, 3, 7, 109
Harbage, A., 10, 11
Hazlitt, W., 55
heaven receive my soul, 108
Heidegger, M., 111, 115
heir apparent, 13, 20, 144
homosexuality, 38, 63
Horatio, 9–10, 18, 24, 33, 38–40, 42–44, 49, 55–58, 68–69, 70–71, 87, 89, 94, 96, 100–101, 106–107, 109, 114
hostility, 66, 73, 76
hour, the ninth, 108
Hoy, C., 1
humanism, Renaissance, 39
humor, gallows, 94
husband
new, 27
second, 35
hyperboles, 64
hysteria, 86, 87

I

I am, I am, 108, 115
I think therefore I am, 115
id, 39
idealization, 108
lost father, of the, 49
identification(s), vi, viii, 40–41, 46–50, 80–81, 91, 99, 108
altruistic, 41, 43
failure of, vii
unconflicted, vii

vicissitudes of, vii
with aggressor, 41, 47
identity (identities), 2, 11, 13, 70
multiple, 52
typological, 93
idiom
Catholic, 48
psychoanalytic, 48
illusion(s), 58, 91, 107, 111
imagery, 73
sexual, 31, 76
visual, 4, 6, 39
images
art, 4
dream, 4
sexual, 76
visual, 4
immortal(ity), 104, 108–109
father's, 46
immortalization, spiritual, 14
imperative(s)
conscious/unconscious, 7
personal, 7
impulse(s), sexual and hostile, 31
inauthenticity, 113
incest, 15, 86
inconsistency (inconsistencies), 4, 6, 7, 10–11, 52, 64, 113
incorporation(s), 46, 147
negative, 47
infidelity, 25, 69, 72
infinite (infinity), 1, 50, 111
instructions, stage, 56
integration, 52, 112–113
pseudo, 87
intention, artistic, 2, 7
internalization, 48, 112
interpretation(s), 2–3, 5–6, 23, 29, 70, 85–86
art, 5, 66
art historical, 5
artistic, 5
critical, 5
directional, 5
dream, 5, 6

of art works, psychoanalytic, 6
psychoanalytic, 5, 58
psychodynamic, 58
Interpretation of Dreams, The, 2–3
interpreter of art
   psychoanalytic, 6
   dream, 6
intimacy, 52, 113
intrigue, court, 23
introject(s) (introjection), 46, 58, 91
   negative, 47
   positive, 47
   regressive, 47
irony (ironies), 14
irrational(ity), 56, 58, 66, 68, 70–71, 90, 111
Isaac, Sacrifice of, the, 20
It is finished, 108

J

Jannings, E., 41
jealousy, 21, 95
Jenkins, H., 3
Jephthah, 64
Jerusalem, 104
Jessica, 83
jester, 96
Jesus, viii, 80, 93, 95, 96, 99, 103–104, 108–109
   appearance of, 108
   death of, 108
   face of, 104
   ministry of, 108
   Passion of (*See also:* Passion Play), vii, 93–94, 99, 107
John
   father of Shakespeare, 3
   St., Gospel of, 108
Jones, E., 2, 102
Jung, C., 111

K

Kernberg, O., 58
king (*See:* Claudius)

King
   Charles I, 7
   Charles II, 5
   Fortinbras, 44, 49, 50
   Hamlet, 9–10, 13–15, 18, 20–23, 25, 30, 32, 38, 44, 50–54, 105
   James, 11
   James Bible, 108
   John, 3
   Lear, 83
Knights, L., 115
Krafft-Ebing, R. von, 41
Kris, E., 3

L

Lady Macbeth, 83
Laertes, 10–12, 17–20, 33–34, 37–38, 40, 58, 88, 90, 93–94, 99–100, 102–106
letter (from Hamlet), 18
Levin, H., 58
Lewis, C., 1, 17
lex talionis, 13
lexicon, 91
   psychoanalytic, 46
   religious, 90
Liebert, R., 3
life, vii, 1, 14, 29, 35, 37, 41, 48, 52, 62, 97, 99, 104, 107, 112, 114–115
   after death (afterlife), 3, 47, 90, 91, 98, 109
   and death, 39, 81, 91, 96, 98, 114
   Everlasting, 109
   in heaven, 91
   inner, 58
linear time frame, 89
Linus's blanket, 112
Lola Lola, 41
loss, 3, 13, 30, 47, 48, 91, 113
love, 35, 41–42, 53, 70, 99, 113
   authentic, 23
   homosexual, 38
   selfish, 23
   sexualized, of the mother, 2, 17
Lucianus, 70
Luke, St., 108

M

mania (manic-depressive disorder), 51
manipulation (manipulator), 37, 38
Mann, H., 41
Mann, T., 41
Marcellus, 10, 55
Mark, St., 80, 108
martyrdom, preordained, 103
Mary, St., 103
masochism, 40, 41
masterpiece, 1, 7, 114
mastery, 3, 57
Matthew, St., 80, 101, 108
meaning(s), viii, 1, 4–5, 38, 48, 62, 88–89, 104, 111–112
   condensed, 5, 108
   Elizabethan, 20
   idiosyncratic, 52
   latent, 4
   meanings, 13
   multiple, 4, 7, 59, 79, 98
   symbolic, 88
meaningful, 58, 70
meaninglessness, 14, 49, 62
means (Hamlet's), 13, 14
medicine, scientification of, 51
memory (memories), 9
   eidetic, 48
Merchant of Venice, The, 83
Mercutio, 38
micropsychosis, 58
mind, 14, 52, 70, 76, 78, 98
   archaic, 12
   deranged, 31
   Elizabethan, viii
   out of control, 67
   reader's, 55
   shattering, 114
   state of, 57
   tormented, 31, 68
Miranda, 83
misery, 32–33, 43, 87
mission, 44, 46, 54
   lethal, 58
model, topographic, 4

monarchy, 7
morality, 94
   Christian, 99
mortal(s), viii
   first, 21, 95
   primal, 104
mortality, 95
Moses, 3, 6, 93, 108, 115
Moses of Michelangelo, The, 3, 4, 6
mother (*See also:* Gertrude), vii, 1–3, 11, 18, 20, 23, 27, 28, 30–32, 35, 49, 52–55, 58, 66, 71–72, 74, 76, 80–81, 83, 86, 97, 104, 106, 112, 114
motivation(s), 47
   for creativity, 3, 7
   unconscious, 13
Mount, Sinai, 93, 108, 115
mourning, vii, 3, 7, 47–48, 90, 108–109
Mousetrap, The, 70
murder, 12–14, 17–18, 25, 29–30, 43, 53–54, 70, 72, 86, 94–95, 103
   brother's, 21
   Claudius's, 14
   father's, 18, 21, 29, 37, 53, 54, 92, 114
   first, 21, 95
   Polonius's, 12, 81
   retaliatory, 13
murderer(s), 13, 32, 44, 69, 70
My god, My god, why has Thou, 108
mysticism, 57

N

nephew, 3, 70
Nero, 72
neurosis (*See:* psychoneurosis)
no more, 98, 107
non sequiturs, 4, 78–79, 87
nonexistence, vii–viii, 52, 98, 111, 112, 114
not being, 98, 108, 114–115
notebook (Hamlet's), 55
nothingness, 99, 101, 108, 111, 113, 115
not-mother, 112
not-self, 112

INDEX

O

O that this too, viii
O what a rogue and, 64
obedience, blind, 89
object
    as interpersonal other, 41, 47, 52, 112, 113
    transitional, 112
o'er-hasty marriage, 23
omega, 108
omnipotence, 37
oneness, sense of, 112
ontogenesis, 111, 48, 113
ontology, psychoanalytic view, 112
Ophelia (*See also:* Scene, Nunnery), 15, 26, 30, 37, 40, 58–59, 68–69, 83–91
    betrayal by, 85–86
    burial of, 10, 33, 39, 99
    death of, 88–89, 94
    deception by, 66, 86
    madness of, 86–87
opportunists, 78
Oremland, E., viii
Oremland, J., 1, 3–5, 112
Origins and Psychodynamics of Creativity, The, 4, 6
Osric, 100, 103–105, 107

P

papist, 11
paradox, vii, 109
    ultimate, 107
paralysis, catatonic, 113
paranoia, 63, 113
parapet (*See also:* Scene, Parapet), 64, 89, 93, 114
parapraxis, 70
Passion Play (*See also:* Christ, Passion of), viii, 93–94, 99, 107
Passover, the, 20
pathography, 3
Pentecost, the, 99, 108
perceptions, 62
Perloff, C., 5
perpetrator, 12–13, 37
perpetuity, 96
personal, the, 6, 7
personality
    borderline, 58
    multiple, 52
personification(s), vii, 16, 39, 93, 104
perversion, sexual, 41
pirates, 18
play within the play, 27, 69, 70
player(s), 14, 64, 65
playwright, 30
plea, 16, 20, 107
plot (to kill Hamlet), 17, 18, 19, 42, 68, 81, 93–94
polarity (polarities), 107
    basic, 98, 113
    good and bad, 113
    life and death, 98, 101
Pollock, G., 3
Polonius, 12, 15, 17, 26, 29, 30, 32, 38, 59, 60, 64, 71, 76, 80–81, 86–88, 90
Portia, 83
pragmatism, 16–17, 32
predestination, 101
preordination(ist), 107–108
presence, inner, 46–47, 49
pride, 16
priest, 10, 99
process, 5–6, 46–48, 60
    paranoid, 63
    primary, 39
    psychotic, 58
    regressive, 5
    rehearsal, 5
    schizophrenic, 53, 87
    secondary, 39
proclamation, 99, 102
    anti-war, 46
procrastination, 46
Professor Unrat, 41
projection, 5–6, 40, 91
Prosser, E., 5, 10, 13–15, 58
psychiatry, 51
psychoanalysis (psychoanalyst), 6, 24, 38, 39, 40, 48, 52, 91

Psychoanalytic Inquiry, vii
psychodynamics (dynamics), vii, 4, 6, 24, 52–53, 58, 86, 111
psychology, academic, 46
psychoneurosis (neurosis), 51, 53, 87, 111
psychopath, amoral, 16
psychosis (madness) (insane) (mental illness), vii–viii, 31, 38, 44, 51–54, 57–60, 62, 64, 67– 69, 75, 77, 79, 81, 84, 86–87, 94, 99–100, 102, 111, 113–114
puppets, 62
Purgatory, 10–11, 14
purposefulness, 49
    cosmic, 101
Pyrrhus, 14

Q

Queen, the (*See:* Gertrude)
question, existential, 98, 115
quotation, Hebrew, 108

R

rage(s), 66, 68, 73, 78, 84
    infantile, 113
rapier(s), 100, 105
rationality (rationalist), 39, 56, 57, 70, 106, 107
rationalization, 14, 57, 65
reality, 41, 44, 55, 99
    interpersonal, 51
    testing, 51
realization, 43, 44, 62, 75–76, 97–98, 111
    mind-shattering, 114
    of death, viii, 98, 109
    of finiteness, viii, 43–44, 80, 98–99
reason(s), 42–43, 45
    political, 28
reasoning, 45
    archaic, 10
    logical, 39

rebirth, 94, 104
redundancy (redundancies), 7, 64
referee, duel's, 104
regicide, 13, 15, 21
regress(ion), 49, 52, 84, 113–114
    ontogenetic, 113
regressive, 44, 47–48, 52, 86, 90, 113–114
reincarnation, 47, 91
reintegration, viii, 50
    of Hamlet, 81, 115
relatedness, interpersonal, 96, 113
religion(s), 7, 48, 91, 98, 111
Remember me, 7
remembrances, loving, 30
remorse, 29
Renaissance, 7, 89
repose, state of, 108
representation (intrapsychic)
    affect laden, 113
    composite, 4
    multilayered, 4
    of self and other, 113
    verbal, 39
repressions, 47, 113
responsiveness, dawning of, 112
Restoration, English, the, 5
Resurrection, 95, 99, 104, 108
return, corporeal, 108
revenge (*See also:* tragedy), 1, 2, 5, 7, 11–14, 17, 20, 37–38, 72, 85, 88, 92–93, 100, 103, 105
reveries, bittersweet, 48
righteousness, 99
rituals
    cannibalistic, 48
    swearing, 57
rivalry, primal sibling, 21
Romeo, 38
Rose, G., 3
Rosencrantz (*See also:* Guildenstern), 42, 60, 61, 63, 71, 78
Rowse, A., 3
rue, 89
rule, golden, 13

S

Sacher-Masoch, L. von, 41
salvation, 16, 93
Santayana, G., 10–11
Sartre, J., 111, 113, 115
Scene
    Closet (*See also:* bed chamber), 25, 27, 35
    Duel, 34, 102–103
    Graveyard, viii, 80–81, 93–94, 97, 104
    Nunnery, 59, 66–68, 84, 86, 89
    Parapet, 64, 93
    Prayer, 13–15, 17
    Swearing, 56
schizophrenia (*See also:* psychosis), vii, 51–53, 58, 60, 62, 65, 74, 87, 113
secret, 17, 32
seduction, 54
seems and seeming, 24–25, 35, 114
self, vii–viii, 6, 15–17, 26–27, 47–50, 53, 55, 64–66, 85, 111–114
    -annihilation, 52, 99
    -cohesion, 41, 52, 113
    -concepts, 52
    -condemnation, 65
    -criticism, 63
    -defense, 113
    -depreciation, 41
    -derision, 65–66
    -differentiation, 52
    -disintegration, 113
    -doubt, 63
    -enhancement, 48–49
    -enhancing, 47–48
    -fragility, 52
    -fragmentation, vii–viii, 52, 87, 113
    -fulfillment, 41
    -integration, 48
    -lambasting, 45
    -loathing, viii, 15, 17
    -preservation, 17
    -proclamation, 102
    -search, 16, 33, 45, 50, 81
    -transcendence, 52
    coalesced, 112
    development of, 52, 111
    dissolution of, vii, 114
    finiteness of, viii
    protean, 24, 26
    states, anachronistic, 113
    states, atavistic, 113
separateness, sense of, 112
series, complementary, 112
serpent, 15
Shakespeare, W., 1–5, 7, 14–15, 39, 49, 54, 64, 68, 74, 83, 89, 94, 96, 108–109, 114–115
shuffled off . . . mortal coil, viii
Schulz, C., 112
Sinai, Mount (Mt. Horeb) (*See:* Mount Sinai)
sister, 1, 18, 37, 88, 102
skull, 94–96, 104
soliloquy, viii, 64–66, 97–98
son, 1, 3, 7, 23, 30, 32, 34–35, 44, 50, 71, 73, 75–76, 81, 93, 95, 99, 109
    dutiful, 37, 49
    first-born, 20, 103
song, foolish, 87–90
soul, 1, 47, 90–91, 108
    Christian, 10–11
    fearful, 11
space, psychic, 112
spirit(s), 47–48, 108
    Christian, 11
    evil, 51
Spirit, Holy, the, 48
splitting (*See also:* schizophrenia), 59, 65
spying, 30
Station
    Fourth, 104
    Sixth, 104
stepfather, 35
Stern, D., 112
stichomythia, 28
sublimations, 113
subscript of Passion Play, 107
subterfuge, 55
subtext in *Hamlet,* viii
succession (successor), 44, 49–50

suicide, 39, 43, 89–90, 94, 97
Summers, M., 10
superego, 48
superstitions, 39
surrender
    altruistic, 41
    utter, 62
swear (*See also:* Scene, Swearing), 56
sword, poisoned, 20
symbol(s), 4, 40, 48, 88–89, 96, 104
symbology, Christian, 103
sympathy, 33, 38

T

taint not thy mind, 14
task
    artist's, 6
    Fortinbras's, 49
    ghost's, 54
    repugnant, 1
    task (Hamlet's), 1, 11, 12, 93
tears, 25
tell my story, 109
Tempest, The, 83
Testament, The New (*See also:* Gospel, the), 104
the very coinage of, 11
The rest is silence, viii, 107–108
theme(s), 1
    Cain–Able, 21
    Christian, 93, 102
    eternal, 94
    political, 7
    revenge, 7
    socioeconomical, 7
Themes of Death and Mourning in Art and Literature, vii
theology, 91, 94
    deistic, 107
    medieval, 10, 39
theophany, 93
    Mosaic, 108
"thing, a", 112
"third, a", 112
thought(s), 59–60, 98–99, 114–115

disorganized, 84
disturbance in, 51
existential, 111
flow of, 59
jangled, 114
of the psychotic, 60
primal, 72
projected, 72
Renaissance, 7
spasms of, 98
tender, 66
twentieth-century, 115
Western, 99
Tidings, Glad, the, 107
timeless(ness), 1, 39
To be or not to be, viii, 24, 66, 98
topical, the, 6, 7
Topper, 11
tradition
    Elizabethan theater, 11
    existential, 16, 115
    psychoanalytic, 91
    theological, 91
tragedy, 33, 35, 43, 81, 86
    revenge, 1–2, 7, 11, 93
transcendence, 7, 113
transformation, 7, 58
trustworthy, 68
truth(s), 53, 80
    essential, 111
    universal, 94, 99
twinship, mystical, 44
typology, 4
typus Christi, 93, 104

U

uncle, 1, 2, 44, 49, 54, 58, 70, 76, 105
unconscious (the), vii–viii, 2, 6–7, 12–13, 15, 48–49, 54, 70, 103, 112
underpinning
    archetypal, 21, 109
    Passion Play, 94
undoing, magical, 12–13
universals (the), 6–7, 48, 94, 99
university, 37

INDEX

unpregnant of my cause, 65
untrustworthy, 53, 77, 81, 114
"utmost, the", 111
utterance
    final, viii
    simple (Hamlet), 98

V

values, 42, 50
    human, 48
    mystical, 39
    transmission of, 48, 91
vase, delicate, 2
vengeance, 37
Venus in Furs, 41
Vere, De, E. (*See:* De Vere, E.)
Veronica, 104
viewer, art, 5, 6, 66
Vinci, da, L. (See: da Vinci, L.)
violets, 40, 89
vision
    Jesus's, viii
    prophetic, 103
visitation, 47, 103
vulnerability (vulnerabilities), 37, 114

W

wager, 100
wake, feast of the, 48
Washburn College Bible, 108
wherefore have you left Me, 108
wife, 23, 53, 70
    (Gonzago's), 80
Wilson, J., 23
wine, poisoned, 20, 105
Winnicott, D., 112
winter, dead of, 89
wish(es), 48–49, 70, 87
    child's, 13
    for continuance, 20
    for death, viii
    infantile, 2, 13
    oral incorporating, 48
    unconscious 54

women, 83
    hatred of, 67, 86
word(s), 13–14, 25, 33–34, 56, 81, 107–108, 115
    agonal (Claudius), 20
    caring (Gertrude), 33
    first, 27
    last, 34, 71, 108
    last (Gertrude), 105
    last (Hamlet), 107, 108
    monosyllabic, 98
    plays on, 59–60, 95
    warmest (Gertrude), 30
work, art (*See:* art work)
World War, II, 111
wound, spear, 104
wretched, 20

Y

Yorick, 30, 96